CU00705463

THE HAPPY
H A N D B O O K

by

Liggy Webb

Grosvenor House
Publishing Limited

Liggy Webb is hereby identified as author of this
work in accordance with Section 77 of the Copyright, Designs
and Patents Act 1988

The book cover picture is copyright to Liggy Webb

This book is published by
Grosvenor House Publishing Ltd
28-30 High Street, Guildford, Surrey, GU1 3HY.
www.grosvenorhousepublishing.co.uk

A CIP record for this book
is available from the British Library

ISBN 978-1-907652-78-3

This book is dedicated to

Kate Tuck

Thank you for everything

Acknowledgements

I would especially like to thank the following people for helping me to make this book happen!

Nick Anderson and my FLF. You fill my world with so much love and happiness.

Lawrence McIlhoney, Andy Veitch, Sara Pankhurst, Jacky Leonard and Melanie Lisney for your constant and greatly appreciated source of unconditional support and encouragement.

My inspirational and loving family Robin and Ann Webb, Jacky Pearson and Charles Christie - Webb.

And to all my fabulous friends who help to make the rich tapestry of my life so vibrant and enchanting.

Thank you.

Just a Thought

Yesterday I had a thought.

That thought became an emotion

That emotion turned into words,
The words fuelled action,

The actions became a habit. My habits are my
Character,

My Character defines my destiny.

Today, therefore, I think

I'll think about my thoughts a little more.

© Liggy Webb

Contents Page

CONTENTS

Introduction

When I first came up with the idea of compiling a book of modern life skills and began my research, I was sharing my vision and concept at lunch with a group of colleagues when someone asked, somewhat scathingly: "So is it going to be *another* one of those *self help* books?".

Quick as a flash, before I even had time to respond, a fellow diner interjected, "Well, what better kind of help is there?".

The lively debate that ensued was enlightening and entertaining and certainly highlighted some of the cynicism that is attached to the plethora of "self help" books that are available to us all now in the twenty tens.

My colleagues debated the merits and pitfalls of books that profess to solve all the problems of modern living and provide a fix it solution to stress, depression and our increasingly demanding life styles. The views and experiences were broad, the attitudes eclectic and the conclusion inconclusive.

For what it's worth, having now digested a virtual library of this genre of books for my research, I can honestly say that I don't bear any real scepticism towards any of them.

I keep an open mind.

Surely, if the content of *any* self help book resonates and helps someone to move in a more positive direction, then who are we to criticise something just because it doesn't necessarily work for us? The phrase "Don't knock it until you have tried it" most certainly springs to mind!

In a world gone slightly mad, with depression affecting more and more people, it seems that there is an increasing need for us to turn our lives around in pursuit of making them happier, healthier and altogether more sustainable. With more emphasis on this and more options available to us on a daily basis, it is little wonder that we become confused about what is best for us.

Consumerism has, of course, jumped on the band wagon and, seemingly without shame, profiteers on the back of the weak and vulnerable. Quick fix solutions are all the rage in a world where speed is of the essence and instant gratification is the way to our hearts and depleting bank accounts.

Personally, I am not convinced that there is a single silver bullet solution to health, happiness and to the greater good of our long term sustainability on Planet Earth. I believe it is more about taking personal responsibility for the choices we make each day of our lives. It is about taking a good look in the metaphorical mirror and challenging our existing habits.

By making more intelligent choices, we can each build our own tailored toolkit of life skills that can positively help us to make the best and most out of our lives.

This book is aimed to keep concepts easy to digest and apply. It is absolutely *not* designed to replace the advice of a medical professional.

The objective is to provide a simple and helpful compendium of life skills that anyone can use. Some may work for you; some may not. One size doesn't fit all because the great news is that we are all unique and special.

My desire is to entertain, provoke thought and look at a holistic approach to life by addressing the physical, psychological and spiritual elements of health and happiness. It is essentially a quirky toolkit of fun tips, techniques, some perceived wisdom, some shared learning and essentially a whole host of positive concepts and happy things.

So, in terms of the original question that was posed to me over lunch with my colleagues quite a while ago, the answer is yes, this book most certainly is about *self help* because isn't that just about the best place to start?

Happy Reading

Liggy Webb

www.liggywebb.com

Modern Life Skills

Life skills are the abilities for adaptive and positive behaviour that enable individuals to deal effectively with the demands and challenges of everyday life

The World Health Organization

The challenges that face us in modern life, such as finding purpose, defining ourselves and managing stress, are numerous and complex. In order to address them effectively, you need practical and useful strategies to help you to be able to cope more positively and effectively.

The United Nations Educational, Scientific and Cultural Organization (UNESCO) divide life skills into subsets of categories which include the following:

Learning to know (cognitive abilities) which involves decision-making, problem-solving and critical thinking skills.

Learning to be (personal abilities) which involves skills for increasing internal control, managing feelings and managing stress.

Learning to live together (interpersonal abilities) which involves interpersonal communication skills, negotiation and refusal skills, empathy, co-operation, teamwork and advocacy skills.

There is however no definitive list of life skills and all of the above includes the psychosocial and interpersonal skills generally considered important. The choice and emphasis on different skills will vary according to the individual and circumstances. Though the list suggests these categories are distinct from each other, many skills are used simultaneously in practice. Ultimately, the interplay between the skills is what produces powerful behavioural outcomes. The Happy Handbook looks at modern life skills that link into each other so that positive behaviours and outcomes can be achieved to promote an altogether happier existence.

The United Nations' subset of categories for life skills lays out an excellent basis to begin with; there are, of course, other life skills that are required to address a more holistic approach to modern living that incorporates the physical, psychological and spiritual aspects of life.

The Happy Handbook - A Practical Guide to Modern Living

Life is what YOU make it!

This book is designed to be an easy read and endeavours to keep the key messages clear, simple, concise and constructive. It is a tool box for you to dip into whenever you need to and choose from it what works best for you.

You will discover information on a range of essential life skills and each one is summarised with useful tips to support you in improving the quality of your life.

There is also an eclectic collection of thought provoking and useful "happy stuff" that includes music, films, quotes and recommended websites to help you to achieve the happy factor.

Overall the aim of The Happy Handbook is to provide you with a positive compendium of modern life skills and tools to help you to thrive in the twenty tens and embrace modern living in the happiest, healthiest and most positive way.

In Pursuit of Happiness

The purpose of our lives is to be happy

Dalai Lama

The Happy Handbook is aimed to help you to live a happier and healthier life. Happiness could well be claimed to be the *master life skill* and we could indeed define it as our purpose as it does appear to be the one that everyone pursues.

To be happy is, in fact, one of our most basic and fundamental desires. So if everyone has always wanted it – and if everyone is actively seeking it – why doesn't everybody have it?

First of all, before I try to define happiness and look at the experts views on the subject, it may well be pertinent to address the topic of depression, something that has been described as the curse of our generation. Many of the life skills that you will encounter in this book will be very useful in helping you to develop a toolkit and coping mechanism in terms of combating some of the symptoms of depression.

According to The World Health Organization, depression will be the second biggest cause of illness worldwide by 2020. The UK mental health charity

MIND claims that one in four of us will experience a mental health problem at some point in our lifetimes, meaning that all of us will either be directly affected or know someone who is.

It is the silent, insidious nature of depression that makes it so hard to measure and can leave those affected feeling like the invisible patient. For those who suffer, it can be one of the most debilitating ailments imaginable. Having personally been challenged with depression, it has provided me with a great deal of empathy and a keen desire to raise awareness of what can positively be done to self-manage and take proactive measures to deal with depression. Having now spent many years researching the subject, with myself as the primary guinea pig, the one major discovery that I have made is that there is always hope and a way through the dark black tunnel. The light we seek at the end does not necessarily depict an oncoming train as we can so readily believe when we plummet into the depths of despair.

For everyone who suffers, it is different. The desire to stay in a darkened room and play dead wrapped and bound in a duvet is overwhelming and a dysfunctional relationship with any addictive substance that can distract or numb the horrible feeling is dangerously tempting and, potentially, highly destructive.

At its most severe, depression can be life-threatening, with nearly a million associated suicides each year worldwide according to the latest World Health Organization statistics.

Depression is a serious illness and still there is huge stigma attached to it. Health professionals use the words depression, depressive illness or clinical depression to refer to it. It is very different from the common experience of feeling miserable or fed up for a short period of time.

Women are twice as likely to suffer from depression as men, although men are far more likely to commit suicide. This may be because men are more reluctant to seek help for depression.

A few people still think that depression is not a real illness and that it is a form of weakness or admission of failure. This is simply not true. Depression is a real illness with real effects, and it is certainly not a sign of failure. In fact, famous leaders, such as Winston Churchill, Abraham Lincoln and Mahatma Gandhi, all had periods of depression.

Later in the book, I will cover managing depression as a life skill as there are many things that individuals who suffer can do to take a proactive approach and improve the quality of their life in order to be happier.

So what is Happiness?

We are taught at a very early age that we are to seek out happiness, yet no one really knows what that is. When we are children, our concept of happiness is minimal. As years pass, our concept of happiness becomes much more expansive. We are schooled to think that, if we succeed at something, whether it is at a career, college or in relationships, we are seeking to be happy. Some people seek out happiness through religion, or a spiritual leader, It seems that everyone has their own idea as to what makes them happy. It becomes ingrained in us that seeking happiness is the point of our existence.

To find happiness, then, we will be living a complete life. What makes happiness or, better yet, where happiness exists is a question that has been pondered by many great thinkers.

Aristotle, the great philosopher, believed that happiness was the meaning and the purpose of life, the whole aim and end of human existence. He believed that we choose happiness always for itself, and never for the sake of something else. It is the end at which all virtuous actions aim. It must be some good, or set of goods that, in itself, makes it worth living.

According to Immanuel Kant, the German philosopher, the road map towards happiness is not so black and white. Kant thought that the means to happiness could not be clearly known. Kant believed there was too much ambiguity in defining personal happiness, thus making it unsuitable as a basis for morality. Kant holds that the pursuit of a person's own happiness or interest is of no moral worth whatsoever. Kant insists that we can never determine whether an action is good or right by considering its effects on one's happiness.

Many of us chase happiness by acquiring material goods; however, scientific studies support the age-old saying that "money doesn't buy happiness". Psychologists David Myers and Ed Diener find that "happiness grows less from the passive experience of desirable circumstances than from involvement in valued activities and progress toward one's goals".

Psychologist Tal Ben-Shahar, in his book *Happier*, defines happiness as "the overall experience of pleasure and meaning". Ben-Shahar describes happiness as the ultimate currency, the end to which all other ends lead, and he says happiness is the indicator by which we measure our lives.

For most of us, happiness is that pleasant feeling we get when life is good. The happiness emotion might be anywhere in the range of feelings from contentment to joy, but we know it when we see it, and we like it.

Psychologist Martin Seligman, author of *Authentic Happiness*, defines a formula for happiness:

$$H = S + C + V$$

... where S is one's happiness set point, C constitutes one's life circumstances, and V is a factor representing a person's voluntary activities. S, a combination of genetic disposition and cultural upbringing, is largely out of our control. C, one's life circumstances, may also be difficult to change.

But V is where we have total control and opportunity. The activities in which we engage and the ways we choose to think about our lives offer each of us the opportunity for greater happiness. As Ralph Waldo Emerson said, "What lies behind us and what lies before us are tiny matters compared to what lies within us."

Psychologists suggest that happiness is not a destination, but a process. Rather than viewing life as a period of necessary hardship and struggle with the promise of happiness at retirement or beyond, we can reasonably strive to find happiness every day of our lives.

Tal Ben-Shahar suggests that we should not ask ourselves if we're happy, but that the better question is "How can I become happier?". This implies there is always the possibility for greater positive feelings, confirming the spiritual teachings of Abraham, urging us to continuously reach for a better feeling in order to attract the good things of life.

So clearly happiness means different things to different people which is why we are all unique and the key is to establish what works best for you and what ultimately feeds your soul.

The Happy Handbook will examine a whole host of component life skills which will help to support you and your journey. The best place to start however, will be to look at how YOU define happiness, what it means to you and how you can personally achieve and sustain it.

> *Happiness resides not in possessions and not in gold. The feeling of happiness dwells in the soul*

Democritus

Further Reading on Happiness

Authentic Happiness by Martin Seligman

Happier by Tal Ben - Shahar

Be Happy by Robert Holden

The Art of Happiness: A Handbook for Living by His Holiness the Dalai Lama and Howard C. Cutler

Happiness: A Guide to Developing Life's Most Important Skill by Matthieu Ricard

Happiness: Lessons from a New Science (Second Edition) by Richard Layard

Happiness Hypothesis: Putting Ancient Wisdom to the Test of Modern Science by Jonathan Haidt

The How of Happiness: A Practical Guide to Getting The Life You Want by Sonja Lyubomirsky

Visit www.liggywebb.com/hh for additional resources.

Happiness - Useful Tips

✓ The first step in being happy is simply to choose to BE happy – It is your choice.

✓ Be limitlessly in love with your life.

✓ You get out of life what YOU put into it.

✓ In finding happiness for others, you will find it for yourself.

✓ Bring happiness to others without harming yourself, and bring happiness to yourself without harming others. Balance is key.

✓ Be kinder than you have to be.

✓ Be tough minded and tender-hearted.

✓ Never pass up the opportunity to tell someone you love them or to rescue a friend in need. Besides, you never know when you will need a strong shoulder or a helping hand.

✓ Love unconditionally. Laugh uncontrollably. Smile endlessly. Live limitlessly.

✓ Find your sense of purpose and be comfortable in your own skin.

✓ It is calmest before the storm and darkest before the dawn. Expect the unexpected, or, ultimately, expect nothing at all. Take it as it comes. You will never be let down.

✓ Moving on does not necessarily mean leaving behind – we all know we can carry people and experiences with us throughout a lifetime.

(Continued on next page)

✓ Remember mistakes aren't mistakes at all – merely learning experiences – the stepping stones to strength and mastery

✓ Anger is like grasping a hot coal with the intent of throwing it at someone else – you are the one who ends up getting burned

✓ Finding humour in any situation is your ultimate key to happiness

✓ You can never truly appreciate the light if it doesn't ever get dark

✓ Take the long, scenic route every chance you get, and realise that time is what life is made of – it is not to be rushed or squandered

✓ Worry not about the past – it is gone; and worry not about the future – it will happen soon enough

Personal Notes & Resolutions

Believe in Yourself

Believe in yourself! Have faith in your abilities!
Without a humble but reasonable confidence in your
own powers you cannot be successful or happy

Norman Vincent Peale

Nelson Mandela included the following inspiring piece of writing in his inaugural speech in South Africa in 1994. It epitomises quite perfectly the need for us to embrace the potential within us confidently and positively.

Our deepest fear is not that we are inadequate. Our deepest fear is that we are powerful beyond measure. It is our light, not our darkness that most frightens us. We ask ourselves, Who am I to be brilliant, gorgeous, talented, fabulous? Actually, who are you not to be? You are a child of God. Your playing small does not serve the world. There is nothing enlightened about shrinking so that other people won't feel insecure around you. We are all meant to shine, as children do. We were born to make manifest the glory of God that is within us. It's not just in some of us; it's in everyone. And as we let our own light shine, we unconsciously give other people permission to do the same. As we are liberated from our own fear, our presence automatically liberates others.

An Extract from - A Return To Love: Reflections on the Principles of A Course in Miracles
by Marianne Williamson

Fear of failure is one of the greatest fears people have and one of the biggest blockages to learning. Fear of failure is closely related to fear of criticism and rejection. Successful people overcome their fear of failure.

The Law of Feedback states that there is no failure; there is only feedback. Successful people look at mistakes as outcomes or results, not as failure. Unsuccessful people look at mistakes as permanent and personal.

So many people limit themselves and don't achieve a fraction of what they are capable of achieving because they are afraid they will fail. You must believe to achieve!

I have not failed. I've just found 10,000 ways that won't work

Thomas Edison

Self Belief - Useful Tips

✓ **Take action** - Action gives you the power to change the circumstances or the situation. You must overcome the inertia by doing something. Dr. Robert Schuller asks: "What would you do if you knew you would not fail?" What could you achieve? Be brave and just do it. If it doesn't work out the way you want, then do something else. But DO SOMETHING NOW.

✓ **Be persistent** - Successful people just don't give up. They keep trying different approaches to achieving their outcomes until they finally get the results they want. Unsuccessful people try one thing that doesn't work and then give up. Often people give up when they are on the threshold of succeeding.

✓ **Be objective** - Don't take failure personally. Failure is not a personality characteristic. Although what you do may not give you the results you want, it doesn't mean YOU are a failure.

✓ **Don't beat yourself up!** If something doesn't work, don't give yourself a hard time; move on; look towards the doors that are just about to open, not at the ones that have just closed.

✓ **Treat failure as a learning opportunity** - You have to be prepared to increase your failure rate if you are to increase your rate of success - Ask yourself the following four questions.

1. What was the mistake?
2. Why did it happen?
3. How could I have prevented it?
4. What will I do BETTER next time?

✓ **Look for the probortunity** - Out of every crisis there is an opportunity and for every problem there is a solution. So seek out the probortunity!

Personal Notes & Resolutions

How You Learn

Learn from yesterday, live for today, hope for tomorrow
Albert Einstein

The ability to learn and to actively do something with what you have learnt is such an important life skill. We can easily amass a great deal of knowledge and information; however, if we don't do something positive with it, then, in some respects, it could be considered a bit of a waste of time! There are many health benefits to learning and more evidence shows the importance of keeping our brain as a goal seeking mechanism, active, interested and receptive.

It is also useful to understand that we are all different and we will learn in different ways. Knowing and understanding your learning style can make a big difference to how well you learn and at what speed. There are so many interesting models about learning; however, here is one of my favourite explanations of the different approaches to learning.

Learning Styles

Auditory or Visual Learners - This indicates the sensory mode you prefer when processing information. Auditory learners tend to learn more effectively through listening, while visual learners process information by seeing it in print or other visual modes including film, picture, or diagram or videos when available.

Applied or Conceptual Learners - This describes the types of learning tasks and learning situations you prefer and find most easy to handle. If you are an applied learner you prefer tasks that involve real objects and situations. Practical, real-life learning situations are ideal for you. If you are a conceptual learner, you prefer to work with language and ideas; practical applications are not necessary for understanding.

Spatial or Non-spatial Learners - This reveals your ability to work with spatial relationships. Spatial learners are able to visualise or "mentally see" how things work or how they are positioned in space. Their strengths may include drawing, assembling things, or repairing. Non-spatial learners lack skills in positioning things in space. Instead they tend to rely on verbal or language skills.

Social or Independent Learners - This reveals your preferred level of interaction with other people in the learning process. If you are a social learner you prefer to work with others – both peers and instructors – closely and directly. You tend to be people-oriented and enjoy personal interaction. If you are an independent learner, you prefer to work and study alone. You tend to be self-directed or self-motivated, and often goal-oriented.

Creative or Pragmatic Learners - This describes the approach you prefer to take toward learning tasks.

Creative learners are imaginative and innovative. They prefer to learn through discovery or experimentation. They are comfortable taking risks and following hunches. Pragmatic learners are practical, logical, and systematic. They seek order and are comfortable following rules.

Multiple Intelligences

It is also useful for us to understand that we are *all* intelligent, however, this can be in different areas – it is not necessarily based on IQ . The theory of multiple intelligences was developed in 1983 by Dr Howard Gardner, professor of education at Harvard University.

It suggests that the traditional notion of intelligence, based on IQ testing, is far too limited. Instead, Dr. Gardner proposes eight different intelligences to account for a broader range of human potential in children and adults. These intelligences are:

Linguistic Intelligence
This area has to do with words, spoken or written. People with high verbal-linguistic intelligence display a facility with words and languages. They are typically good at reading, writing, telling stories and memorising words along with dates. They tend to learn best by reading, taking notes, listening to lectures and discussion and debate.

They are also frequently skilled at explaining, teaching and oration or persuasive speaking. Those with verbal-linguistic intelligence learn foreign languages very easily as they have high verbal memory and recall, and an ability to understand and manipulate syntax and structure. This intelligence is highest in writers, lawyers, philosophers, journalists, politicians, poets and teachers.

Logical-Mathematical Intelligence
This area has to do with logic, abstractions, reasoning and numbers. It is often assumed that those with this intelligence naturally excel in mathematics, chess, computer-programming and other logical or numerical activities.

A more accurate definition places emphasis on traditional mathematical ability and more reasoning capabilities, abstract patterns of recognition, scientific thinking and investigation, and the ability to perform complex calculations. It correlates strongly with traditional concepts of "intelligence" or IQ. Many scientists, mathematicians, engineers, doctors and economists function on this level of intelligence.

Visual-Spatial Intelligence
This area has to do with vision and spatial judgment. People with strong visual-spatial intelligence are typically very good at visualising and mentally manipulating objects. Those with strong spatial intelligence are often proficient at solving puzzles. They have a strong visual memory and are often artistically inclined.

Those with visual-spatial intelligence also generally have a very good sense of direction and may also have very good hand-eye co-ordination, although this is normally seen as a characteristic of bodily-kinaesthetic intelligence. Careers that suit those with this intelligence include artists, engineers and architects.

Bodily-Kinaesthetic Intelligence
This area has to do with bodily movement. People who have this intelligence usually learn better by getting up and moving around, and are generally good at physical activities such as sports or dance. They may enjoy acting or performing, and in general they are good at building and making things. They often learn best by doing something physically, rather than reading or hearing about it.

Those with strong bodily-kinaesthetic intelligence seem to use what might be termed muscle memory and they remember things through their body such as verbal memory or images. Careers that suit those with this intelligence include football players, athletes, dancers, actors, surgeons, doctors, builders and soldiers.

Musical Intelligence
This area has to do with rhythm, music, and hearing. Those who have a high level of musical-rhythmic intelligence display greater sensitivity to sounds, rhythms, absolute pitch and music. They normally have good pitch and may be able to sing, play musical instruments, and compose music.

Since there is a strong auditory component to this intelligence, careers that suit those with this intelligence include instrumentalists, singers, conductors, disc-jockeys, orators, writers and composers.

Interpersonal Intelligence
This area has to do with interaction with others. People who have a high interpersonal intelligence tend to be extroverts, characterised by their sensitivity to others' moods, feelings, temperaments and motivations, and their ability to cooperate in order to work as part of a group.

They communicate effectively and empathise easily with others, and may be either leaders or followers. They typically learn best by working with others and often enjoy discussion and debate. Careers that suit those with this intelligence include politicians, teachers, managers and social workers.

Intrapersonal Intelligence
This area has to do with introspective and self-reflective capacities. They are usually highly self-aware and capable of understanding their own emotions, goals and motivations. They often have an affinity for thought-based pursuits such as philosophy. They learn best when allowed to concentrate on the subject by themselves.

There is often a high level of perfectionism associated with this intelligence. Careers that suit those with this intelligence include philosophers, psychologists, theologians, writers and scientists.

Naturalist Intelligence
This area has to do with nature, nurturing and relating information to one's natural surroundings. Those with it are said to have greater sensitivity to nature and their

place within it, the ability to nurture and grow things, and greater ease in caring for, taming and interacting with animals. They may also be able to discern changes in the weather or similar fluctuations in their natural surroundings. Recognising and classifying things are at the core of a naturalist.

They must connect a new experience with prior knowledge to truly learn something new. Naturalists learn best when the subject involves collecting and analysing, or is closely related to something prominent in nature; they also don't enjoy learning unfamiliar or seemingly useless subjects with little or no connections to nature. It is advised that naturalistic learners would learn more through being outside or working in a kinaesthetic way. Careers that suit those with this intelligence include vets, environmentalists, scientists, gardeners and farmers.

Dr. Gardner believes that our schools and culture focus most of their attention on linguistic and logical-mathematical intelligence. We esteem the highly articulate or logical people of our culture. However, Dr. Gardner says that we should also place equal attention on individuals who show gifts in the other intelligences: the artists, architects, musicians, naturalists, designers, dancers, therapists, entrepreneurs and others who enrich the world in which we live.

The theory of multiple intelligences proposes a major transformation in the way our schools are run. It suggests that teachers be trained to present their lessons in a wide variety of ways using music, co-operative learning, art activities, role play, multimedia, field trips, inner reflection, and much more.

So while this information is quite a lot to absorb in one sitting, it is useful to be aware of how you learn best and why so that you can choose the learning channels that work most effectively for you.

Happy Learning.

> *Anyone who stops learning is old,*
> *whether at twenty or eighty*

Henry Ford

Recommended Reading on Learning

Learning for Life: The Foundations of Lifelong Learning by David H. Hargreaves

Learning for Life in the 21st Century: Sociological Perspectives of the Future by Gordon Wells and Guy Claxton

Learning Through Life: Inquiry into the Future for Lifelong Learning by Tom Schuller and David Watson

Learning for Life: From Inspiration to Aspiration by over 250 young people in Scotland and David Lorimer

Visit www.liggywebb.com/hh for additional resources.

Changing Your Behaviours

*Habits are at first cobwebs
and then they become cables*

Spanish Proverb

Our daily lives are often a series of behaviours played out through the day, a trammelled existence fettered by the slow accumulation of our previous actions.

The human brain is a magnificent machine and consists of billions of nerve cells with innumerable extensions. This interlacing of nerve fibres and their junctions allows a nerve impulse to follow a number of routes known as neural pathways. When you learn something new, your brain makes connections that create new pathways for activity. Setting up neural pathways is actually quite simple. If a newly-learned behaviour is repeated enough times, it eventually gets programmed into the subconscious mind; that behaviour becomes automatic and we no longer have to think about doing it, because we respond automatically. This, simply put, is a habit.

Have you ever arrived at home or work with no memory of how you got there? When you started on your journey, you thought about the first few steps on that familiar path but, somewhere along the way, your brain moved onto more interesting topics, and the next thing you knew, you'd arrived. This is the essence of habits: once you start on a familiar series of actions, you stop thinking about them and you are able to complete them without conscious thought or attention.

Cache memory in a computer is another good analogy. The computer stores commonly-used actions where it can access and process them faster. The brain does the same thing. This can work in both a positive and negative way as it can free up our minds from dull or repetitive tasks, although it also makes it difficult to stop once we've started.

Over 90% of our daily routine is comprised of various habits that create our behaviours. What separates the positive and negative people is that the positive people have habits and behaviours that are conducive to success, while the negative people have ones that facilitate failure in their lives. Remember: you control your habits - they do not control you. Your life is the culmination of all the daily behaviours that you have. You are where you are right now because of the behaviours that you have adopted in the past.

It is important to identify which habits in your life lead to negative consequences and which lead to positive rewards. The difficulty in this sometimes has to do with instant gratification. If you change your habits, on occasions you're not going to see an immediate effect. It is for this reason that people struggle with diets or can't stop drinking, smoking, or spending money because they can't control the instant gratification that is delivered.

Experts in hypnosis and NLP (Neuro-Linguistic Programming, which is the art and science of personal excellence) believe that it takes around 21 to 28 days to form the basis of a new habit or behaviour. The time it takes to replace an old one is inconclusive because it depends entirely on the person and how long they have owned it.

As with any newly learned behaviour, you may well experience some internal resistance for the first week or more. This is natural and it's not going to be easy, so you have to mentally prepare for this challenge ahead of time. After you survive this first week, you will find that your new habit and behaviour becomes easier and easier to do and soon you don't even have to think about doing it at all.

> *We first make our habits, and*
> *then our habits make us*

John Dryden

Changing Habits - Useful Tips

✓ **Do just one habit at a time** - This is really important. Habit change is difficult, even with just one habit. If you do more than one habit at a time, you're setting yourself up for failure. Keep it simple, allow yourself to focus, and give yourself the best chance for success.

✓ **Take the 30-day Challenge** - Allowing about 30 days to change a habit is a good starting point if you're focused and consistent. This is a round number and will vary from person to person and habit to habit.

✓ **Write it down** - Just saying you're going to change the habit is not enough of a commitment. You need to actually write it down, on paper. Write what habit you're going to change.

✓ **Make a plan** - This will ensure you're really prepared. The plan must include your reasons and motivations for changing, obstacles, triggers, people who will support you, and other ways you're going to make this a success.

✓ **Understand your motivations** - Be sure they're strong. Write them down in your plan. You have to be very clear why you're doing this, and the benefits of doing it need to be clear in your head.

✓ **Write down all your obstacles** - If you've tried this habit change before and it hasn't worked, reflect on those failures, and work out what stopped you from succeeding. Write down every obstacle that's happened to you, and others that are likely to happen.

(Continued on next page)

Then write down how you plan to overcome them. That's the key: write down your solution *before* the obstacles arrive, so you're prepared.

✓ **Identify your triggers** - What situations trigger your current habit? For the smoking habit, for example, triggers might include waking in the morning, having coffee, drinking alcohol, stressful meetings, going out with friends, driving, etc. Most habits have multiple triggers. Identify all of them and write them in your plan.

✓ **Ask for help** - Get your family and friends and co-workers to support you. Ask them for their help, and let them know how important this is.

✓ **Become aware of self-talk** - You talk to yourself, in your head, all the time — but often we're not aware of these thoughts. Start listening. These thoughts can derail any habit change, any goal. Often they're negative: "I can't do this. This is too difficult. Why am I putting myself through this? How bad is this for me anyway? I'm not strong enough. I don't have enough self discipline." It's important to know you're doing this.

✓ **Stay positive** - You will have negative thoughts — the important thing is to realise when you're having them, and push them out of your head and then replace them with a positive thought.

✓ **Prepare for the saboteurs** - There will always be people who are negative, who try to get you to do your old habit. Be ready for them. Confront them, and be

(Continued on next page)

direct: you don't need them to try to sabotage you, you need their support, and if they can't support you then you don't want to be around them.

✓ **Use visualisation -** This is powerful. Vividly picture, in your head, successfully changing your habit. Visualise doing your new habit after each trigger, overcoming urges, and what it will look and feel like when you're done.

✓ **Reward yourself** - You might see these as bribes, but actually they're just positive feedback. Put these into your plan, along with the milestones at which you'll receive them.

✓ **Renew your commitment often -** Remind yourself of your commitment hourly, and at the beginning and end of each day. Read your plan. Celebrate your success. Prepare yourself for obstacles and urges.

✓ **Bounce back -** If you fail, work out what went wrong, plan for it, and try again. Don't let failure and guilt stop you. They're just obstacles, but they can be overcome. In fact, if you learn from each failure, they become stepping stones to your success. Regroup. Let go of guilt. Learn. Plan. And get back on that road to success!

Personal Notes & Resolutions

Assertiveness

Assertiveness is not what you do, it's who you are

Cal Le Mon

Assertive communication is an excellent interpersonal skill to develop. It is the ability to express your thoughts and opinions while respecting the thoughts and opinions of the other person. Assertive communication is appropriately direct, open and clarifies your needs to the other person. Assertiveness is a skill that can be learned. People who have mastered the skill of assertiveness are able to greatly reduce the level of interpersonal conflict in their lives and significantly reduce a major source of stress.

Being assertive is being able to communicate appropriately in an honest way. When we allow the needs, opinions or judgment of others to become more important than our own, we may feel hurt, anxious and even angry. This kind of behaviour is often indirect, emotionally dishonest and self-denying.

Many people feel that if they attend to their legitimate needs and assert their rights they are being selfish. Selfishness, however, is being concerned with only our own rights, with little or no regard for others. Implicit in our rights is the fact that we are concerned about the legitimate rights of others as well.

Assertiveness is sometimes seen as the mid-point between passive and aggressive ways of being. Understanding the different way in which we communicate is important and I have outlined the following ways in which different people choose to put their message across

Being passive

Being passive may be a response to feeling that we must be "nice" people. We may become compliant, believing that certain behaviours will lead to our being judged and rejected, or we may fear confrontation and become anxious to avoid this. Passive behaviour can be perceived as manipulative and may elicit a care-taking, non-challenging response in others.

Being aggressive

Being aggressive may be a response to feeling powerless or insecure or it could be the behaviour of a dominant social style. Aggressive behaviour may be any behaviour which gives us power over others. It may take the form of threats, bullying, sarcasm, fighting etc. It is likely to elicit a defensive or aggressive response from others.

Behaving passive-aggressive

Sometimes this can happen when we keep feelings locked inside, leading to a state of resentment. If we are always "nice", this can leave us feeling that we are often exploited. If the build-up gets too much, we may get to a point where we explode inappropriately or at the wrong target. We may also say nothing and internalise our anger however creating an atmosphere around us and ill feeling within ourselves.

Behaving assertively
This is by far the most healthy way to communicate because it is about being honest and respectful with ourselves and with others. It is about putting our point across in open way that may well encourage confidence in others. People generally feel more secure and comfortable around assertive people as they command trust and confidence. Look at some of the greatest communicators and the common denominator is their ability to assert themselves.

It is important to connect to our feelings and use them to help us recognise what we want to change. It will help if we can express our emotions to an appropriate person in a non-blaming way. Communicating our feelings gives us a chance to be better understood or improve our relationships.

Brooding too long over an incident is only likely to make matters worse. Non-assertive people often assume others should be able to spot their hurt or anger even though they don't say what they feel.

We can set clear boundaries by learning to say no without apologising unnecessarily. Excuses, apologies and explanations may be superfluous. Whilst knowing that our agenda is important, it is helpful to take time to hear another's point of view and to remember that it is not always possible to get what we want.

Change does not happen overnight, and others may react differently to us as we change. Learning to be assertive is about experimenting with new ways of communicating and having the courage to put your message across appropriately, respectfully and with confidence.

> *The only healthy communication style*
> *is assertive communication*

Jim Rohn

Recommended Reading on Assertiveness

Assertiveness and Diversity by Anni Townend

Assertiveness Step by Step (Overcoming Common Problems) by Windy Dryden and Daniel Constantinou

Assertiveness at Work: A Practical Guide to Handling Awkward Situations by Ken Back and Kate Back

The Assertiveness Pocketbook (The Pocketbook) by Max Eggert and Phil Hailstone

Easy Ways to Build Assertiveness, Confidence and Self-Esteem by Jennie Willett

Visit www.liggywebb.com/hh for additional resources.

Assertiveness - Useful Tips

✓ Believe in yourself and other people

✓ Assertiveness doesn't mean you always win

✓ Be an effective and active listener

✓ State limits and expectations

✓ Observe without labelling or judging

✓ Express yourself directly and honestly

✓ Be aware of other people's feelings

✓ Avoid judging people

✓ Trust yourself and others

✓ Behave in a trustworthy way

Personal Notes & Resolutions

Change Ability

*It is not the strongest of the species that survives,
or the most intelligent, but rather the one most
adaptable to change*

Charles Darwin

Life in the twenty tens has seemingly propelled us into a rapidly changing world where the escalating pace of change is greater today than at any other time in our recorded history. Every aspect of our lives is changing including the way that we work, the way that we communicate, the way that we shop and eat and, for the majority, the entire way that we live our day-to-day lives.

Unlike in the past it is more the norm to change not only jobs, but often entire careers, several times. People now think nothing of re-locating, not only within their own country but also internationally. And it is now common for more and more people to be married more than once and have more than one family. It's as if we are trying to fit several lifetimes into one.

Never before have so many people needed to deal with so many life changing decisions, in so many different life areas, on such a consistent and accelerating basis. And one of the great challenges of our times is the ability to cope with change.

As the saying goes, the only people who seem to like change are busy cashiers and wet babies. We find change disorienting, creating within us an anxiety similar to culture shock, the unease visitors to an alien land feel because of the absence of the familiarity they took for granted back home. With an established routine, we don't have to think!

We do, however, feel better about the changes that we know or believe are going to make us better off in some way, but the changes that we are uncertain of, or believe may be detrimental, are, for many people, their greatest fear. Generally, people fear the changes that they feel they cannot steer. The great paradox, that so many people live in, is that they want things in their life to get better, while at the same time being resistant to change.

In reality, the only future thing of which we can be absolutely certain is that there will be continuing change in all of our lives. At times, the changes may be only minor while, at other times, they will be major, but all of us will experience some degree of change. It is inevitable. You cannot stop it! You cannot even slow it or delay it. What you can do however, with a little knowledge, skill and effort, is to learn how to direct it. Learning how to consciously direct, the natural changes of life towards your heartfelt desires, is most definitely a very important modern life skill.

Change is, in fact, a vital criterion for any form of evolution or growth, whether as individuals or as an entire community, society, country or world. Without change there can be no movement or growth, either personal or global.

Just as nature is in an ever-continuing cycle of change, so we, as part of nature, are constantly changing. Continuing change is not only a certainty of life but also necessary for our own growth, evolution and general wellbeing.

Change is like the wind that blows. It is neither good nor bad, friend or foe, it just is, and will continue to be. It would be naïve to expect the wind to never blow again or for change to not occur.

A small minority of people in every age have discovered this great truth and have learned how to benefit from the winds of change. Great leaders, inventors, pioneers, innovators, and builders, in fact every great success, in any area of life, will have been achieved in some way through learning to adapt successfully to change and embrace the potential it can bring.

Change is happening faster than ever before and, in the process, it is creating numerous opportunities. We live in unique, special and exciting times and our ability to adapt to change will be our greatest life skill.

> *Be the change you want the world to be*

Mahatma Ghandi

Recommended Reading on Change Ability

I Ching, the Book of Changes by Yi Jing

The Life of Mahatma Ghandi by Louise Fischer

Thinking for a Change by John C .Maxell

Managing Change (Essential Managers) by Robert Heller

Managing Change and Transition (Harvard Business Essentials) by Harvard Business Essentials

Managing Change Step by Step: All You Need to Build a Plan and Make it Happen by Richard Newton

Visit www.liggywebb.com/hh for additional resources.

Change Ability - Useful Tips

✓ Be willing and open to change

✓ Change little things every day

✓ Understand the feelings change brings

✓ Keep some things the same

✓ Be around positive people

✓ Find out the reasons behind the changes

✓ Understand the transition process

✓ Don't take change personally

✓ Take responsibility for your own change management

Personal Notes & Resolutions

Communication

*The single biggest problem with communication
is the illusion that it has been achieved*

George Bernard Shaw

Communication occurs when someone understands you, not just when you speak, and one of the biggest dangers in communication is that we spend more time on transmit than we do on receive. We can, if we are not careful, work on the assumption that the other person has understood the message that we are trying to get across - and that's when communication breaks down.

It is a lot easier to see something from our own perspective and much more difficult to look at it from another person's, especially when we all have different personalities, backgrounds, ideas, beliefs and values.

Poor communication can lead to negativity, insecurity, bitching, back-stabbing and blame which, in turn, can also affect our stress levels, especially when we don't understand something or feel that we have been misled. Communication can also have a very positive effect when it works well and can make people feel valued, respected and even loved.

The development of communication has provided us, in the last few decades, with a whole new range of media including email, instant messaging, the internet and mobile phones. All of these items undeniably enhance our communication. However, if misused, these gadgets can create issues and pose problems.

The danger we have is that, with more and more consumer-driven technological toys being created, we are starting to shut out real people in our everyday lives.

Clearly, if we continue to bypass face-to-face communication, our interpersonal skills will suffer as a result. Most human beings need personal interaction. We are social creatures and thrive on cultivating and developing relationships with others. We are now running the danger of alienating ourselves – and some of the old traditional means of face-to-face communication are now sadly being lost entirely.

Professor Albert Mehrabian pioneered the understanding of communications in the 1960s. Aside from his many and various other fascinating works, Mehrabian established this classic statistic for the effectiveness of face-to-face communication. His findings concluded the following:

• 7% of meaning is in the words that are spoken.

• 38% of meaning is in your tone of voice.

• 55% of meaning is in non verbal communication.

Mehrabian's model has become one of the most widely referenced statistics in communications.

The theory is particularly useful in explaining the importance of meaning, as distinct from words.

The value of Mehrabian's theory relates to communications where emotional content is significant, and we need to understand it properly in order to mitigate the risk of misunderstandings. This is so important in the workplace, where motivation and attitude have a crucial effect on outcomes.

Understanding the difference between words and meaning is a vital capability for effective communications and relationships.

The understanding of how to convey when speaking and interpret when listening will always be essential for effective communication, management and relationships.

Transferring Mehrabian's findings to emails and telephone conversations, for example, is simply to say that greater care needs to be taken in the use of language and expression, because the visual channel does not exist.

It is fair to say that email and other written communications are limited to conveying words alone. The way that the words are said cannot be conveyed, and facial expression cannot be conveyed at all. Mehrabian provides us with a reference point as to why written communications, particularly quick, reduced emails and memos, so often result in confusion or cause offence.

Understanding how we communicate and the impact that it can have on people is really important and there are many ways that we can see to improve our communication skills.

> *Wise men talk because they have something to say; fools, because they have to say something*

Plato

Recommended Reading on Communication

Nonverbal Communication by Albert Mehrabian

Relationship of Verbal and Non-verbal Communication (Contributions to the Sociology of Language)
by Mary Ritchie Key

Power in Language: Verbal Communication and Social Influence (Language and Language Behavior)
by Sik H. Ng and James J. Bradac

The Handbook of Communication Skills by Owen Hargie

The Jelly Effect: How to Make Your Communication Stick by Andy Bounds

What Every Body Is Saying: An Ex-FBI Agent's Guide to Speed-reading People by Joe Navarro

The Definitive Book of Body Language: How to Read Others' Attitudes by Their Gestures
by Allan Pease and Barbara Pease

Visit www.liggywebb.com/hh for additional resources.

Communication - Useful Tips

✓ Communicate positively

✓ Actively listen and focus

✓ Understand your communication style

✓ Use open gestures and body language

✓ Be supportive to those around you

✓ Use humour appropriately and respectfully

✓ Be an assertive communicator

✓ If in doubt, check your understanding

✓ Encourage feedback about your communication

✓ Smile - it is the universal currency in communication

Personal Notes & Resolutions

Conflict Resolution

Conflict is inevitable, but combat is optional

Max Lucade

Conflict is when two or more values, perspectives and opinions are contradictory in nature and haven't been aligned or agreed about yet. This could indeed be with yourself when you're not living according to your values or when your values and perspectives are threatened. It can also involve discomfort from fear of the unknown or from lack of information.

In life, conflict is inevitable and, if managed effectively, it can be a positive thing and beneficial. For example, good teams always go through a "form, storm, norm and perform" period. Getting the most out of diversity means handling often-contradictory values, perspectives and opinions.

Physiologically, we respond to conflict in one of two ways. We either want to "get away from the conflict" or we are ready to "take on anyone who comes our way". Think for a moment about when you are in conflict. Do you want to leave or do you want to fight when a conflict presents itself? Neither physiological response is good or bad, it's just a personal response. What is important to learn, regardless of our initial physiological response to conflict, is that we must intentionally choose our response to conflict.

Whether we feel like we want to fight or flee when a conflict arises, we can deliberately choose a conflict mode. By consciously choosing a conflict mode we are more likely to productively contribute to solving the problem at hand.

Conflict can be really positive as it helps to raise and address problems and can energise the focus to be on the most appropriate issues with a view to resolution and results. It also helps people "be real" and motivates them to participate as well as helping then to learn how to recognise and benefit from their differences.

Conflict is not the same as discomfort. The conflict isn't the problem – it is when conflict is poorly personally managed that is the problem. Conflict is a problem when it hampers productivity, lowers morale and causes continued conflicts that lead to negative, disruptive and inappropriate behaviours.

All sorts of things cause conflict from poor communication, not being informed about changes and not understanding another person's motivation. We may not understand the reasons for decisions which can lead to misinformation and rumours, which is very unsettling. Disagreement about "who does what" and stress from trying to deal with inadequate resources can be a real agitation.

We will, of course, experience personality clashes, because not everyone is like us and it can be frustrating when someone doesn't get our point of view. We can also rub each other up the wrong way and often what we don't like in others is what we actually don't like in ourselves.

In conflict we also need to control our emotions and try to not get angry or aggressive. Anger is often stress in denial and some angry people take pride in their anger and don't want to change; others fail to appreciate the effect it has on themselves and on others. Without a commitment to change, there's not a lot that can be done, anger management is only possible when an angry person accepts and commits to change.

A big factor in persuading someone of the need to commit to change and manage their anger is to look objectively and sensitively with the other person at the consequences (for themselves and others) of their anger. Often angry people are in denial ("my temper is okay") and put it down to acceptable mood swings and the frustration at the situation as opposed to the way that they are choosing to handle it. Helping angry people to realise that their behaviour is destructive and negative is an important first step. Most importantly recognising how you handle your own emotions is key and taking responsibility to manage them is mastery.

Trying to be as objective as possible and focusing on the benefits of resolving conflict is far more positive and conducive to happy living. After all, life is rather too short for unnecessary confrontation and so much better when we resolve our differences and move on from them in a positive and constructive way.

The greatest conflicts are not between two people but between one person and himself

Garth Brooks

Recommended Reading on Conflict Management

Tongue Fun By Sam Horn

The Resolving Conflict Pocketbook (Management Pocketbooks) by Max Eggert and Phil Hailstone

Comebacks at Work: Using Conversation to Master Confrontation by Kathleen Reardon and Christopher T. Noblet

Managing Conflict in Organizations by M.Afzalur Rahim

Visit www.liggywebb.com/hh for additional resources.

Conflict Resolution - Useful Tips

✓ Tell yourself to remain calm

✓ Diffuse your own or the other persons anger

✓ Listen to what the other person has to say

✓ Genuinely consider the other person's point of view

✓ Try to put yourself in their shoes

✓ Try to gain all the facts and information

✓ If you are wrong, quickly admit it and take responsibility

✓ Draw on positive past experiences to apply

✓ Use visualisation to imagine a positive outcome

✓ Once the situation is resolved – let it go!

Personal Notes & Resolutions

Coping with Grief

Death leaves a heartache no one can heal,
love leaves a memory no one can steal

A headstone in Ireland

Grief is the most painful of all human experiences and is a very natural reaction to loss. It is the process which allows people to come to terms with the loss and resulting change in their lives. Loss can take many forms, from the obvious death of a partner, relative or friend, to divorce or the loss of a job.

Grief is a very personal and individual experience and is composed not of just one feeling, but of many. However, though we may experience different feelings at different times, grief usually follows a general, recognisable pattern. Losing someone or something you love is very painful. After a significant loss, you may experience all kinds of difficult and surprising emotions, such as shock, anger, and guilt. Sometimes it may feel like the sadness will never end. While these feelings can be frightening and overwhelming, they are normal reactions to loss. Accepting them as part of the grieving process and allowing yourself to feel what you feel is necessary for healing.

There is no right or wrong way to grieve. However, there are healthy ways to cope with the pain. Grief that is expressed and experienced has a potential for healing that eventually can strengthen and enrich life.

Grief is a natural response to loss. It's the emotional suffering you feel when something or someone you love is taken away. You may associate grief with the death of a loved one – and this type of loss does often cause the most intense grief.

Grieving is a personal and highly individual experience. How you grieve depends on many factors, including your personality and coping style, your life experience, your faith, and the nature of the loss. The grieving process takes time. Healing happens gradually; it can't be forced or hurried – and there is no "normal" timetable for grieving. Some people start to feel better in weeks or months. For others, the grieving process is measured in years. Whatever your grief experience, it's important to be patient with yourself and allow the process to naturally unfold.

In 1969, psychiatrist Elisabeth Kübler-Ross introduced what became known as the "five stages of grief". These stages of grief were based on her studies of the feelings of patients facing terminal illness, but many people have generalised them to other types of negative life changes and losses, such as the death of a loved one or a break-up.

The Five Stages of Grief

Denial - In the denial stage we refuse to believe what has happened. We try in our mind to tell ourselves that life is as it was before our loss. We can even make believe to an extent by re-enacting rituals that we used to go through with our loved one.

Anger - We get angry. The anger can manifest itself in many ways. We can blame others for our loss. We can become easily agitated, having emotional outbursts. We can even become angry with ourselves.

Bargaining - This can be with ourselves or, if you are religious, with your god. Often we will offer something to try to take away the reality and pain of what has happened.

Depression - Depression is a very likely outcome for all people that grieve for a loss. This is what I would consider the most difficult stage of the five to deal with. There can be a feeling of listlessness and tiredness. You may be wandering around in a daze, thinking that you are feeling numb, or feeling guilty, as if everything is your own fault. You may find you feel like you are being punished.

Acceptance - The final stage of grief. It is when you realise that life has to go on. You may still have thoughts of your loved one, but less intense and less frequent. You can here accept your loss. You should now be able to regain your energy and goals for the future. It may take some time to get here, but you will.

> *Perhaps they are not the stars, but rather openings in Heaven where the love of our lost ones pours through and shines down upon us to let us know they are happy*

Author Unknown

Recommended Reading on Coping with Grief

On Grief and Grieving: Finding the Meaning of Grief Through the Five Stages of Loss by Elisabeth Kübler-Ross and David Kessler

An Introduction to Coping with Grief by Sue Morris

Coping with Grief: A Self-help Guide by C. A. Komar

First Steps Through Bereavement by Sue Mayfield

Visit www.liggywebb.com/hh for additional resources.

Coping with Grief - Useful Tips

✓ Turn to friends and family members

✓ Draw comfort from your faith

✓ Join a support group

✓ Talk to a therapist or grief counsellor

✓ Avoid alcohol and stimulants

✓ Face your feelings

✓ Express your feelings

✓ Look after your physical health

✓ Don't let anyone tell you how to feel

✓ Plan ahead for grief "triggers"

Personal Notes & Resolutions

Creativity

Creativity involves breaking out of established patterns in order to look at things in a different way

Edward de Bono

Creativity is a very common term these days and is a useful tool when we are not able to solve problems or we need to explore new and innovative ways of doing things. It is also something that we need to do to cut back on some of our costs in challenging economic times!

I am sure that we all unanimously agree on one thing: the fact that problems can be the curse of the day and destroy our peace and happiness. Successful is the one who can conquer their problems and live a happy life. Creativity greatly helps us solve problems in practically all fields. It is also a great way for us to explore a wide range of options that may be open to us and to discover new things.

Creativity is an inborn talent of all human beings and one that can also be learned. It is our creativity that makes us distinct and sets us apart from other animals in this world. It is because of creativity that we are the most successful being on this planet. When we face challenges and aren't able to solve them in the conventional way, we knowingly or unknowingly seek creative solutions. In fact, in many ways, the more creative we are the more successful we can be.

Whatever our profession may be, creativity is something that can make us more successful and make our work easier and more exciting. Here are a few tips that can help us think creatively.

Brainstorming or "mind showers" as they are sometimes called these days can be an effective way to generate ideas on a specific topic and then determine which idea is the best suited solution. It is also a good practice that, whenever you see an idea, criticise it or appreciate it according to your opinion. Don't be overtaken about what others think about the idea, see what you liked about it and appreciate it. Criticise the negative points in the idea. This will make your brain seasoned to good and bad ideas and, next time you are trying to solve a problem, your brain will try to solve it in the way you classify "good" and try to avoid "bad" routes to the solution.

Giving a lot of free time for your mind is an excellent approach. Forget all worries and tensions for some time every day and listen to music that you like or play with children. Avoid TV as it makes you more tired. When we are relaxing, the mind is actually working and putting together things that we were thinking of throughout the whole day. It will come out with creative solutions only if we give it enough time and rest. Always pondering over endless problems keeps our minds occupied and prevents creativity.

Getting stuck to one way of thinking and trying repeatedly the same methods is a common phenomenon among us. Try for a fixed duration to solve the problem. If it doesn't get solved, stop thinking of the problem itself. Relax and get engaged in something else that you have to do. Attend to the problem after some time, or maybe the next day if you have lots of time to find a solution to the problem. You will observe that your mind views the problem at a different angle now and a solution may come out in a flash.

One of the best methods to use is "The Six Thinking Hats" which is a creative thinking system that Edward de Bono designed as a practical user-friendly way of thinking creatively and effectively. It is fun and effective and many people use it.

Creativity can be a huge amount of fun and help you to explore things that you would most likely have never experienced before. It can, at times, take us out of our comfort zone and challenge us. However it is also very good for us to use creative thinking to keep our brains fresh, stimulated and alert so there are indeed lots of benefits to this approach.

> *Creativity is inventing, experimenting, growing, taking risks, breaking rules, making mistakes, and having fun*

Mary Lou Cook

Recommended Reading on Creativity

Six Thinking Hats by Edward de Bono

How to Have Creative Ideas: 62 Exercises to Develop the Mind by Edward De Bono

The Art of Creative Thinking: How to be Innovative and Develop Great Ideas by John Adair

Creativity by Mihaly Csikszentmihalyi

Visit www.liggywebb.com/hh for additional resources.

Creativity - Useful Tips

✓ Listen to classical music

✓ Always carry a small notebook with you

✓ Go for a walk to stimulate the mind

✓ Read as much as you can about everything possible

✓ Exercise your brain with puzzles

✓ Talk to creative people

✓ Play board games

✓ Invent something

✓ Make a collage from old magazines

✓ Switch off the TV and think

Personal Notes & Resolutions

Decision Making

Decision is like a sharp knife that cuts straight and clean, indecision a dull one that hacks and tears and leaves ragged edges

Graham Gordon

All of us have to make decisions every day. Some decisions are relatively straightforward and others are definitely more difficult. Simple decisions usually need a simple decision-making process. Difficult decisions, however, typically involve a whole host of complex issues. Often there is uncertainty where many facts may not be known and you may have to consider many interrelated factors. There are decisions, too, that have high-risk consequences, and the impact of the decision may be significant for yourself and for others. Every given situation has its own set of uncertainties and consequences, and anything that involves interpersonal issues can often be challenging as it difficult to predict how other people will react.

With these challenges in mind, the best way to make a complex decision is to use an effective process. A systematic approach will usually lead to consistent, high-quality results, and can improve the quality of almost everything we do.

A logical and systematic decision-making process can help you to address the critical elements that result in a good decision. By taking an organised approach, you're less likely to miss important factors, and you can build on the approach to make your decisions better and better.

To create a constructive environment for successful decision making, you need to first of all establish your objective and define what you want to achieve. Once you have done this you will need to agree on the process and know how the final decision will be made, including whether it will be an individual decision or involve others. If you have to involve others it is so important to involve the right people and allow other opinions to be heard. Make sure, too, that you are asking the right questions and challenge yourself. Being creative will help too as the basis of creativity is thinking from a different perspective so this is good to do when you are first faced with the situation so that you can explore all your options.

The more good options you consider, the more comprehensive your final decision will be.

When you generate alternatives, you force yourself to dig deeper, and look at the problem from different angles. If you use the mindset "there must be other solutions out there", you're more likely to make the best decision possible. If you don't have reasonable alternatives, then there's really not much of a decision to make!

When you're satisfied that you have a good selection of realistic alternatives, then you'll need to evaluate the feasibility, risks and implications of each choice.

In decision making, there's usually some degree of uncertainty, which inevitably leads to risk. By evaluating the risk involved with various options, you can determine whether the risk is manageable. Risk analysis helps you look at risks objectively. It uses a structured approach for assessing threats, and for evaluating the probability of events occurring.

After you have evaluated the alternatives, the next step is to choose between them.

With all of the effort and hard work that goes into evaluating alternatives and deciding the best way forward, it's easy to forget to "sense check" your decisions. This is where you look at the decision you're about to make dispassionately, to make sure that your process has been thorough, and to ensure that common errors haven't crept into the decision-making process.

Once you've made your decision, it's important to explain it to those affected by it, and involved in implementing it. The more information you can give to people about why you made a certain decision, the better. One of the key benefits of taking the systematic approach to decision making is that you will be able to analyse and evaluate your decision making process which will, in turn, make it easier to communicate.

If you need support of others they will also feel more reassured that you have given consideration to your actions.

This will also give you personal reassurance that you have thought something through without making a knee-jerk decision. Once you have made your decision, accept that you have made the best decision based on the all information that you had a the time. Deliberation or indecision will hamper your progress so go for it and trust in a positive outcome.

> *In any moment of decision, the best thing you can do is the right thing, the next best thing is the wrong thing, and the worst thing you can do is nothing*

Theodore Roosevelt

Recommended Reading on Decision Making

Harvard Business Review on Decision Making ("Harvard Business Review" Paperback) by Harvard Business School Press

Decision Making and Problem Solving Strategies - Creating Success series: 66 by John Adair

Making Difficult Decisions: How to be Decisive and Get the Business Done by Peter J. A. Shaw

The Decision-making Pocketbook (Management Pocketbooks) by Neil Russell-Jones and Phil Hailstone

Visit www.liggywebb.com/hh for additional resources.

Decision Making - Useful Tips

✓ Identify your objective

✓ Create the right kind of environment

✓ Establish who else is involved

✓ Explore the alternatives

✓ Analyse your options

✓ Conduct a risk assessment

✓ Conduct a "sense check"

✓ Make your decision and stick to it

✓ Be assertive in how you communicate it

✓ Believe in a positive outcome

Personal Notes & Resolutions

Emotional Resilience

Our greatest glory is not in never falling,
but in rising every time we fall

Confucius

You have most likely heard the expression "what doesn't kill you makes you stronger" and you may well have experienced that in your own life. Clearly, some people have the ability to spring back from difficulties and trauma more successfully than others. Learning to be emotionally resilient can certainly be a very useful life skill, especially as it is highly likely that we will all experience adversity from time to time in our lives.

The American Psychological Association reports that "emotional resilience" is the process of adapting well in the face of adversity, trauma, tragedy, threats, or even significant sources of stress such as family and relationship problems, serious health problems or workplace and financial stressors. Resilience is "bouncing back" from difficult experiences. Research has shown that resilience is ordinary, not extraordinary, and that people commonly demonstrate resilience. One example is the response of many Americans to the attacks of September 11, 2001 and people's efforts to rebuild their lives.

Being resilient does not mean that a person doesn't experience difficulty or stress. Emotional pain and sadness are common in individuals who have suffered major adversity or trauma in their lives. In fact, the road to resilience is likely to involve considerable emotional distress. Emotional resilience is not a trait that people either have or do not have. The National Institute of Mental Health reports that emotional resilience involves behaviours, thoughts, and actions that can be learned and developed in anyone.

Good relationships with close family members, friends or others is important. Accepting help and support from those who care about you and will listen to you strengthens emotional resilience. Some people find that being active in civic groups, faith-based organisations or other local groups provides social support and can help with reclaiming hope. Assisting others in their time of need also can benefit the helper.

You can't change the fact that highly stressful events happen, but you can change how you interpret and respond to these events. Try looking beyond the present to how future circumstances may be a little better. Note any subtle ways in which you might already feel somewhat better as you deal with the situation.

Certain goals may no longer be attainable as a result of adverse situations. Accepting circumstances that cannot be changed can help you focus on circumstances that you can alter.

Acting on adverse situations as much as you can and taking decisive actions, rather than detaching completely from problems and stresses and wishing they would just go away, is good.

People often learn something about themselves and may find that they have grown in some respect as a result of their struggle with loss. Many people who have experienced tragedies and hardship have reported better relationships, a greater sense of personal strength even while feeling vulnerable, an increased sense of self-worth, a more developed spirituality and a heightened appreciation for life.

Staying positive and developing confidence in your ability to solve problems and trusting your instincts helps build resilience. Even when facing very painful events, try to consider the stressful situation in a broader context and keep a long-term perspective. Avoid blowing the event out of proportion. You also need to pay attention to your own needs and feelings. Engage in activities that you enjoy and find relaxing. Exercise regularly. Taking care of yourself will help to keep your mind and body primed to deal with situations that require resilience and strength.

Optimism is your window to opportunity and can be learned and nurtured over a period of time. An optimistic outlook enables you to expect that good things will happen in your life. Try visualising what you want, rather than worrying about what you fear.

It is also very useful to develop some realistic goals for yourself. Doing something regularly, even if it seems like a small accomplishment, will help you to move positively towards your goals. Instead of focusing on tasks that seem unachievable, ask yourself, "What's one thing I know I can accomplish today that helps me move in the direction I want to go?"

There really are some wonderful examples of how people react to some quite extreme situations that are both heart-warming and encouraging. Human beings most certainly are quite extraordinary creatures and, on occasions, we can surprise ourselves with the strength and potential we possess. If we believe that we have the capacity to be able to deal with even the most extreme situation we can not only develop our own internal resources and confidence; we can also be an inspiration and provide hope for others.

You desire to know the art of living, my friend?
It is contained in one phrase: make use of suffering

Henri Frederic Amiel

Recommended Reading on Emotional Resilience

Emotional Resilience: Simple Truths for Dealing with the Unfinished Business of Your Past by David Viscott

The Power of Resilience: Achieving Balance, Confidence, and Personal Strength in Your Life by Robert Brooks and Sam Goldstein

Managing Change with Personal Resilience: 21 Keys for Bouncing Back & Staying on Top in Turbulent Organizations by Linda Hoopes and Mark Kelly

Control and Surviving in Difficult Times by Dr John Nicholson and Jane Clarke

Visit www.liggywebb.com/hh for additional resources.

Emotional Resilience - Useful Tips

✓ Analyse your reactions to everything

✓ Embrace challenges and change

✓ Take Action – No matter how small

✓ Be open to learning about yourself

✓ Believe in positive outcomes

✓ Maintain Perspective

✓ Look After Yourself

✓ Be positive and optimistic

✓ Set goals and objectives

✓ Be determined and tenacious

Personal Notes & Resolutions

Empathy & Understanding

*People will forget what you said,
people will forget what you did, but people
will never forget how you made them feel*

Bonnie Jean Wasmund

Empathy and understanding is the emotional process that builds connection between people. It is a state of perceiving and relating to another person's feelings and needs without blaming, giving advice or trying to fix the situation. Empathy also means "reading" another person's inner state and interpreting it in a way that will help the other person and offer support and develop mutual trust.

To truly empathise and understand another individual is an intuitive act where you give complete attention to someone else's experience and push aside your own issues. To be truly empathetic is to help another person feel secure enough to open up and share their experience. By being empathetic and understanding, you will make the other person feel that they are not entirely isolated in their predicament and provide them with a safe haven to recover and grow stronger knowing they have a compassionate supporter.

Empathy is different from sympathy. When someone is sympathetic, it also implies support; however it is a feeling that is more fuelled by pity and an emotional distance is maintained from the other person's feelings. An empathetic and understanding approach is more about truly sensing or imagining the depth of another person's feelings. It implies feeling *with* a person, rather than feeling sorry for a person.

Empathy is a translation of the German term *Einfühlung*, meaning to feel as one with. It implies sharing the load, or "walking a mile in someone else's shoes", in order to appropriately understand that person's perspective.

Having a rich capacity for empathy and understanding is not only a great life skill, it is also a wonderful quality if it is used in the right way. It is an ability that can be used for good, or for evil. Once you understand someone you can use that understanding to help them, to heal them, to hurt them or to destroy them. If you reject the skill of empathy, you reject the ability to really understand your fellow humans as well as you could. In war, a lack of empathy can lead to defeat, in justice it can lead to injustice and in relationships it can kill love.

One thing to be aware of is that unless people can extend compassion, empathy, and understanding to themselves, they won't be able to genuinely extend it to others. Not having authentic empathy and understanding for yourself can leave you feeling lonely or alienated; it can also lead to feeling isolated and depressed. Those who are not in touch with their own feelings are likely to have an inhibited sense of conscience. They will find it hard to relate to another person's suffering and also find it very difficult to connect and relate, which, in turn, will make them feel inadequate and potentially angry and dismissive. I am sure we have all experienced people who have little ability to empathise and will label a sensitive person as "too sensitive" and the question I would ask would be "too sensitive for whom?".

For those of us who have the ability to empathise, it is important also to try to understand people who are unable to, and to try to understand that these people may be dealing with some psychological pain of their own and a coping mechanism is to shut their feelings down internally and externally.

The ability to positively empathise and understand is indeed to extend the hand of kindness.

So wouldn't it be great if we could all do this and seek to understand rather than always to be understood. Wouldn't it be a much happier and healthier world if we developed our ability to show sensitivity to other peoples' thoughts and feelings and learned to be more compassionate and empathetic?

> *If there is any one secret of success, it lies in the ability to get the other person's point of view and see things from his angle as well as your own*

Henry Ford

Recommended Reading on Empathy & Understanding

101 Activities for Empathy & Awareness (101 Activities & Ideas) by Sue Jennings

The Compassionate Brain: How Empathy Creates Intelligence by Gerald Huther

The Age of Empathy: Nature's Lessons for a Kinder Society by Frans De Waal

Listening With Empathy: Creating Genuine Connections with Colleagues Clients and Customers by John Selby

Visit www.liggywebb.com/hh for additional resources.

Empathy & Understanding - Useful Tips

✓ Listen – truly Listen to people

✓ Be genuinely interested in what they feel

✓ Don't interrupt

✓ Tune into their body language

✓ Be aware of your body language and vocal tone

✓ Use peoples' names

✓ Be fully present when you are with people

✓ Smile and use eye contact

✓ Encourage quieter people when they open up

✓ Give constructive feedback

Personal Notes & Resolutions

Environmental Awareness

We do not inherit the earth from our ancestors;
we borrow it from our children

Native American Proverb

Environmental awareness is about becoming more aware of the fragility of our environment and fully acknowledging the relationship between the environment and mankind and taking positive action to do something about it. The way we treat our environment is becoming increasingly important and altogether more alarming.

Consumerism certainly plays a large hand in promoting a mentality of instant gratification whilst raping and wasting the earth's resources without any apparent remorse.

Whilst so many people in the world are starving, in western society we throw away a third of the food we buy, a shocking and vulgar statistic.

The suggestion would be that we all become a steward of the land and our natural resources. Collectively we each take or use only what we need to live, and survive. Communities adopt a conserve and preserve mentality, creating an environment that is able meet the needs of present and future generations.

How we live our lives impacts the Earth, both on a global and local level. Taking personal responsibility for the way we treat our environment is key and, if everyone makes a sustainable commitment to do their bit, it could, by critical mass, make a huge impact.

The development of a sustainable environment is possible through long-term planning and vision. Sustainability is essential to our world's health. Long-term planning and vision means eco-friendly development in local communities, which can lead to positive growth in economies.

Our environment is complex and very fragile. It is made up of air, water, land, organic, non-organic matter and living organisms. When one small part of our eco system is contaminated, such as water, the contamination sends out ripples felt by all. Contaminated water affects plants, insects, fish and, eventually, it affects our food chain.

Climate Change

Climate change has long-since ceased to be a scientific curiosity, and is no longer just one of many environmental and regulatory concerns. It is a growing crisis with economic, health and safety, food production, security, and other dimensions.

Shifting weather patterns, for example, threaten food production through increased unpredictability of precipitation, rising sea levels contaminate coastal freshwater reserves and increase the risk of catastrophic flooding, and a warming atmosphere aids the pole-ward spread of pests and diseases once limited to the tropics.

The news to date is bad and getting worse. There is alarming evidence that important tipping points, leading to irreversible changes in major ecosystems and the planetary climate system, may already have been reached or passed. Ecosystems as diverse as the Amazon rainforest and the Arctic tundra, for example, may be approaching thresholds of dramatic change through warming and drying. Mountain glaciers are in alarming retreat and the downstream effects of reduced water supply in the driest months will have repercussions that transcend generations.

The potential for runaway greenhouse warming is real and has never been more present. The most dangerous climate changes may still be avoided if we transform our hydrocarbon-based energy systems and if we initiate rational and adequately-financed adaptation programmes to forestall disasters and migrations at unprecedented scales. The tools are available, but they must be applied immediately and aggressively.

Environmental awareness is essential to the sustainable health of our environment for current and future generations. Natural resources are part of everyone's daily life. If natural resources continue to be depleted then every part of our lives will be detrimentally effected

By taking responsibility and initiative ourselves, we can actively encourage others to be an active participant in taking better care of our planet and our environment.

There are many great initiatives that the UNEP (United Nations Environmental Programme) have set up and many other organisations have implemented campaigns and initiatives to support the environment. You don't have to be an eco-warrior to make a difference; you just need (in the words of Ghandi) to be the change that you would want the world to be.

Only when the last tree has died and the last river been poisoned and the last fish been caught will we realise we cannot eat money

Cree Indian Proverb

Recommended Reading on Environmental Awareness

The Green Book: The Everyday Guide to Saving the Planet One Simple Step at a Time by Elizabeth Rogers

The Big Green Book by Ian Winton and Fred Pearce

Evicted by Anthony Bjorklund

Everything Kids' Environment Book by Sheri Amsel

Environmental and Economic Impacts by Marc J. Epstein

Good to Green: Managing Business Risks and Opportunities in the Age of Environmental Awareness by John-David Phyper

Visit www.liggywebb.com/hh for additional resources.

Environmental Awareness - Useful Tips

✓ Don't buy too much food

✓ Switch off lights and equipment

✓ Unplug your chargers

✓ Print responsibly

✓ Recycle wherever possible

✓ Walk rather than drive

✓ Wrap up in the winter

✓ Buy green electricity

✓ Buy an eco car

✓ Reduce your materialism

Personal Notes & Resolutions

Energy Management

And what is a man without energy?
Nothing - nothing at all

Mark Twain

What are your energy levels like? Are you "ready to go" in the morning? Are you able to maintain high levels of energy throughout the day? Do you rely a lot on caffeine or sugar to keep you going? Do you have much energy at the end of the day?

During the day we all go through stages of feeling up and down, feeling awake and feeling sleepy, being alert and being distracted. Our bodies go through a repeating energy cycle (ultradian rhythms) every 90 to 120 minutes. The implications are that we only do solid work for up to about 90 minutes at a time and we then need a break or switch to something lighter.

The trick to managing your daily energy is to work on the more difficult things when you are alert and focused, and work on the easier stuff (or take a break) when you're feeling lower in energy. To make the most of your time, work in short bursts or sprints and then recover. To maximise your energy, you need breaks.

One good tip is to get up and get going in the morning. The brain is a goal seeking mechanism and likes to get going once we are awake so, if we refuse the snooze on our alarm, we will embrace our day already more energised.

Typically, everything we do either builds or takes away from our energy reserves. Effective time usage depends on looking after multiple sources of energy. These include physical, emotional and mental energy.

Eating well with plenty of vegetables and fruit and being light on the fats and sugars is important, as is making sure you are hydrated by drinking sufficient water. A good slow carbohydrate-releasing breakfast like porridge is excellent for sustaining energy levels. Sugar-rich food will give you a quick energy fix but will leave you feeling even more tired later on.

Exercise is an excellent energiser – I saw a strap-line in my gym that said: "Energy – the more you give the more you get" which, I thought, sums up exercise very well. People who exercise regularly are likely to live longer and enjoy a better quality of life.

Regular exercise also improves mental and emotional health. The chemicals and hormones that are released in the brain through exercise can help deal with stress, promote wellbeing and provide us with more sustainable energy.

Cultivating good relationships with those you live and work with is really important as constant conflict can really drain energy resources. Learning to forgive and not hold onto grudges is really helpful, otherwise they will eat you up and consume not only your energy but your time as well.

Learning to chill out and relax and let go of worry and stress at the end of the day is key. By keeping a clear conscience so that you can relax in the knowledge that you have stuck to your values and principles is one way of being able to clear your mind of anxiety.

Stress can affect sleeping patterns, and poor quality sleep will most definitely affect energy levels. If you are worried about something, it can often be on your mind even when you try to forget about it. This may cause sleepless nights or bad dreams. You may find it difficult getting to sleep or you may wake up a few times during the night. This can also make you tired and groggy the next day.

With regards to mental energy, it is important to be careful with what we feed our minds with, as negative thinking can be a real drain and we can be our own energy saboteurs. We need to learn to switch off so that our mind and body has time to recharge, so some kind of meditative activity would be good, even if it just going for a walk, having a hot bubble bath or spending more time with loved ones.

> *Enthusiasm finds the opportunities and energy makes the most of them*

Henry S. Haskins

Recommended Reading on Energy Management

Instant Energy Boosters by Jan Pleshette

The Optimum Nutrition Bible by Patrick Holford

The Promise of Sleep by William C.Dement

Fit Home Team: The Posada Family Guide to Health, Exercise, and Nutrition the Inexpensive and Simple Way by Bernie Williams, Jorge Posada, and Laura Posada

Fitness For Dummies by Suzanne Schlosberg and Liz Neporent

Visit www.liggywebb.com/hh for additional resources.

Energy Management - Useful Tips

✓ Refuse the snooze on your alarm

✓ Always eat breakfast

✓ Drink 2 litres of water a day

✓ Exercise for 30 minutes every day

✓ Take a walk in the fresh air

✓ Develop healthy sleeping patterns

✓ Reduce caffeine and refined sugar

✓ Live by your values and principles

✓ Take breaks every 90 minutes

✓ Visualise yourself in an energised state

Personal Notes & Resolutions

Goal Setting

Man is a goal-seeking animal. His life only has meaning if he is reaching out and striving for his goals

Aristotle

Goals unlock your positive mind and release energies and ideas for success and achievement. Without goals, you simply drift and flow on the currents of life. With goals, you fly like an arrow, straight and true to your target. Setting goals gives us direction, purpose and focus in our lives.

There are lots of benefits to setting goals. First and foremost, they help you to develop clarity which is the first step to helping you achieve what you want in life.

You will develop a stronger FOCUS: whatever you focus on, you get more of; if you have clear goals and focus on them, you will get more of what you do and want and less of what you don't want.

When you get clear about where you want to go, you set up steps and actions to get there. This increases your efficiency because you are working on what is really important. When you work on what's important, you will accomplish more than you ever expected.

You will get what you really want in life, rather than settling for "whatever comes your way".

As you set and reach goals, you become more confident in your ability to do what you say and get what you want in life. Success breeds more success.

Only 3% of people have proper written goals, and according to research, these people accomplish 80% more than those who don't. That's an astounding difference, isn't it?

A common acronym in goal setting is the possibly-familiar SMART goals, but what does it really mean and what is so smart about them?

The SMART acronym is used to describe what experts consider to be "good" goal statements because they contain most of the essential ingredients. Out of all the formulas I have come across for objective and goal-seeking, it is by far the best and the most easy to apply and stick to.

The SMART acronym itself has several different variations depending on who you ask. However, I think it is useful to look at all of them because it provides a well-rounded goal statement.

S - Specific & significant

M - Measurable, motivational, methodical & meaningful

A - Action-oriented & achievable

R - Realistic, relevant & recorded

T - Time-bound & tangible

The main reason that your brain needs goals is that it behaves as a goal-seeking mechanism, similar to a precision-guided missile. As these missiles fly, they continually make small adjustments and corrections to their trajectories to realign themselves to their target.

Your brain also works in a similar way. Dr Maxwell Maltz, author of the classic *Psycho-Cybernetics*, said that human beings have a built-in goal-seeking "success mechanism" that is part of the subconscious mind.

This success mechanism is constantly searching for ways to help us reach our targets and find answers to our problems. According to Maltz, we work and feel better when our success mechanism is fully engaged going after clear targets.

All we have to do to use this mechanism is to give it a specific target. Without one, our success mechanism lies dormant, or worse, pursues targets we didn't consciously choose.

The key with goal setting is to assertively take control of what we want and to identify exactly what it is that we really want to achieve with a clear understanding of why we want to.

The benefits of goal setting and goal achievement are numerous. It allows you to become more empowered and altogether more responsible for your own destiny and personal success. It also helps to boost your self-esteem and self-confidence which, in turn, has many physical, emotional and mental health benefits.

> *I don't want to get to the end of my life and find that I have just lived the length of it. I want to have lived the width of it as well*

Diane Ackerman

Recommended Reading on Goal Setting

Goal Setting: How to Create an Action Plan and Achieve Your Goals (Worksmart) by Susan B Wilson and Michael S Dobson

Setting Goals: Expert Solutions to Everyday Challenges (Harvard Pocket Mentor) by Harvard Business School Press

Make Success Measurable: A Mindbook-Workbook for Setting Goals and Taking Action by Douglas K. Smith

High Performance Goal Setting: Using Intuition to Reach Your Goals by Beverly A. Potter

Visit www.liggywebb.com/hh for additional resources.

Goal Setting - Useful Tips

✓ Embrace the benefits of what you want to achieve

✓ Set goals that are personal to you and that you are committed to

✓ Understand specifically what it is you want to achieve

✓ Know how to measure your goals

✓ Ensure that your goals are achievable

✓ Write your goals down

✓ Make sure that you set timelines

✓ Use positive affirmations

✓ Believe in yourself

✓ Don't give up

Personal Notes & Resolutions

Healthy Living

*A man too busy to take care of his health is like
a mechanic too busy to take care of his tools*

Spanish Proverb

Your body is an amazing machine. Your heart beats, your blood goes around, your lungs breathe and your digestive system merrily gurgles away. Most of the time, especially when we are younger, we don't even need to think about all those bodily functions and we take them for granted. However, as we grow older, we become increasingly aware of how important it is to look after our bodies, especially as we are now living longer and physical preservation is a key consideration.

First of all, let's get one thing straight – there is nobody on this planet who is exactly the same as you. There are many principles that apply to us all as members of the human race , for example, we all need to move and fuel ourselves to keep going; however, to what extent will vary from each individual. You are essentially the evolutionary dynamics that you have inherited from your parents and the genetically-inherited strengths and weaknesses. The complex interaction of these factors ensures that each individual is born unique although clearly similar to other people.

Understanding ourselves and what works best for us is the first step to better health and personal performance. There are however some key aspects of exercise and nutrition that are fundamental to all of us.

The lack of physical activity is probably the greatest reason why obesity figures are rising. You need to increase your physical activity if you want to lose weight; however, exercise is also good for your all-round health and wellbeing.

Remember too that exercise helps you to make a very positive investment for your future. While we worry about our pensions and make provision materially do we also consider whether we are going to be healthy and active enough in later life to enjoy our retirement. We are living longer these days – therefore our long term health is an increasingly concerning issue.

No matter who you are or where you live, the very fact that you are alive depends on you eating and keeping hydrated. Even the sight and smell of food can trigger the release of a pleasurable and rewarding chemical called dopamine in your brain.

However, while a delicious meal and a drink can be one of the most satisfying sensory experiences, it is also responsible for some of our greatest health problems.

You are essentially what you eat. Each human being is made up of roughly 63 per cent water, 22 per cent protein, 13 per cent fat and 2 per cent minerals and vitamins. Every single molecule comes from the food you eat and the water you drink. Eating the highest quality food in the right quantities helps you to achieve your highest potential for health, vitality and freedom from disease.

However, many people who believe that they have a healthy, well-balanced diet with all the necessary nutrients are misguided. Part of the problem is propaganda and consumerism. It is not easy in today's society (in which food production is inextricably linked to profit). Refining foods makes them last longer, which makes them more profitable yet, at the same time, deficient in essential nutrients.

Nothing in Western society really teaches us to be healthy (apart from any wisdom that our parents may impart). The media has embarked upon many well-intentioned health campaigns; however, so many mixed messages are now sent out about what is good for you, and what is not, that many of us are left in a state of confusion about what constitutes a healthy, well-balanced diet.

The key really is to keep it simple and the fundamentals of weight management is not rocket science. It simply equates to calories in (food) versus calories out (exercise). We also know that drinking plenty of water has numerous health benefits and keeps us hydrated and energised. Whilst we cannot get it right all the time and we are surrounded by temptation, a good approach is to apply the 80/20 rule and if we can get it right 80% of the time then that is fantastic!

> *Health is a state of complete physical, mental and social well-being, and not merely the absence of disease or infirmity*

World Health Organization, 1948

Recommended Reading on Healthy Living

The "Feel Good Factory" on Healthy Living: Life-boosting, Stress-beating, Age-busting Ways to Total Health by Kate Cook etc and Elisabeth Wilson

The 10 Secrets of 100% Healthy People: Some People Never Get Sick and are Always Full of Energy? Find Out How! by Patrick Holford

Healthy Living Made Easy: The Only Things You Need to Know about Diet, Exercise and Supplements by K. St Whiting Ph.D.

Your Secret Laws of Power: The Modern Art of Healthy Living by Alla Svirinskaya

Visit www.liggywebb.com/hh for additional resources.

Healthy Living - Useful Tips

✓ Start each day with a hot water and lemon

✓ Drink herbal and green teas instead of caffeinated drinks

✓ Aim to drink 2 litres of water a day

✓ Never skip breakfast

✓ Avoid refined sugar

✓ Avoid refined carbohydrates

✓ Snack on fruit, vegetables, nuts and seeds

✓ Avoid drinking alcohol every day

✓ Exercise at least 30 minutes a day

✓ Wear a pedometer and do 10,000 steps each day

Personal Notes & Resolutions

Impact and Influencing

*Think twice before you speak, because your words
and influence will plant the seed of either
success or failure in the mind of another*

Napoleon Hill

Making a positive impact and having the ability to influence people is a very powerful life skill to possess. More and more, in the competitive world we live in, having the confidence to stick your head above the parapet and get noticed is very helpful, not just in a work environment but on a personal level as well.

The key is to make the best impact that you can have on people's lives and to be conscious that all of our actions bear consequences. Let's work on the principle that we are all a mass of energy and if we hurt another person we in turn will hurt ourselves. Treating people how we would want to be treated is important and having respect for fellow man is indeed a virtue. If kindness was a religion, the world would certainly be a healthier and happier place.

We can, however, seek out ways to make a positive impact and, by generating enthusiasm and energy, we can add value and help influence others to feel good about themselves and feel more empowered.

Self-confidence (and remember there is a fine line between confidence and arrogance) will breed confidence in others. The greatest leaders in the world have one thing in common and that is a sense of purpose and self-belief. We have looked at some of the very positive benefits of assertive communication earlier in *The Happy Handbook* and assertiveness, both non-verbally and verbally, is the key to making an impact.

So, once you have made a positive impact, you will find it far easier to influence and persuade people because they will already be on your side. Influencing is an important skill to have. However, it is important that you establish first of all what you are trying to achieve. If you are unclear about your own intentions or direction, it will just confuse other people and they will, in turn, lose confidence in where you are trying to take them.

Influence, by definition, is about having a power and power over others, so it is important that you use this power with integrity and due diligence. One of the key skills when influencing is to listen actively and make sure that you have all the facts around you so that you are well informed and are responsibly leading people in the direction you want to take them and toward the outcomes that you want to achieve. Demonstrating empathy and understanding will also help to get people on your side and make them feel far more part of the process, as opposed to being bamboozled or railroaded into something that they may resent later.

A good amount of planning and preparation will help to keep you focused and also demonstrate to those around you that you are trying to influence that you are in control and that you know what are you are doing. If an idea or suggestion has been well thought through it will have far more gravitas.

An openness and honesty about the merits and pitfalls of a suggestion can be very positive too, as this provides a reality check and acknowledges and pre-empts any doubts that anyone may have. They will be more receptive to being influenced if the pros and cons have been weighed up and they have all the facts.

The more you make someone involved and part of the process, the more they will be on your side. Also remember one of the key skills of a influencing is the enthusiasm you convey when delivering any message. A passion, energy and strong belief in what you are trying to achieve can be contagious and the best way to positively impact on and influence others.

> *You don't have to be a "person of influence" to be influential. In fact, the most influential people in my life are probably not even aware of the things they've taught me*

Scott Adams

Recommended Reading on Impact & Influencing

Persuasion – The art of influencing people by James Borg

Personal Impact: What it Takes to Make a Difference by Amanda Vickers, Steve Bavister, and Jackie Smith

21 Dirty Tricks at Work – How to Win at office Politics by Colin Gautrey & Mike Phipps

Influence – The Psychology of Persuasion by Robert B.Cialdini

The Impact and Presence Pocketbook (Management Pocketbooks) by Pam Jones, Jane Van Hool and Phil Hailstone

Influencing within Organizations by Andzrej Huczynski

Visit www.liggywebb.com/hh for additional resources.

Impact and Influencing - Useful Tips

✓ Be enthusiastic and positive

✓ Be confident, energised and assertive

✓ Be patient; influencing is a process

✓ Listen actively, to gain knowledge

✓ Be flexible and adapt to other peoples' ideas

✓ Build, link and develop ideas together

✓ Show understanding for others in order to establish common ground

✓ Express yourself fluently – with passion and facts

✓ Check everyone has understood – to ensure people are with you

✓ Plan and be well prepared

Personal Notes & Resolutions

Listening Skills

I listened, motionless and still; and,
as I mounted up the hill, the music in my heart
I bore, long after it was heard no more

William Wordsworth

Listening is one of the most underrated life skills and yet one of the most powerful. When you fully engage and actively listen, you can learn so much and yet, at times, we spend more time on transmit than we do on receive. You tend to find that people are either interesting (good talkers) or interested (good listeners). The real trick here is to be able to develop a blend of both.

Listening and understanding what others communicate to us is the most important part of successful interaction and vice versa. When a person decides to communicate with another person, they do so to fulfil a need. The person wants something, feels discomfort, has feelings or thoughts about something. In deciding to communicate, the person selects the method or code which they believe will effectively deliver the message to the other person. The code used to send the message can be either verbal or nonverbal. When the other person receives the coded message, they go through the process of decoding or interpreting it into understanding and meaning. Effective communication exists between two people when the receiver interprets and understands the sender's message in the same way the sender intended it.

We were given two ears but only one mouth, because listening is twice as hard as talking. Listening can be challenging; we can become preoccupied and not listen because our internal voice is having a little chat with us. Some people are so interested in getting their point across that they just wait for a gap in the conversation so that they can jump in with their bit.

We can also get so bogged down with own personal beliefs about what is being said that we don't remain objective and listen to the whole message.

There are essentially three modes of listening. These include competitive or combative listening, which happens when we are more interested in promoting our own point of view than in understanding or exploring someone else's view. We either listen for openings to take the floor, or for flaws or weak points we can attack. As we pretend to pay attention, we are impatiently waiting for an opening, or internally formulating our rebuttal and planning our devastating comeback that will destroy their argument and make us the victor.

Another is passive or attentive listening, where we are genuinely interested in hearing and understanding the other person's point of view. We are attentive and passively listen. We assume that we heard and understand correctly, but stay passive and do not verify it.

Active or reflective listening is the single most useful and important listening skill. In active listening, we are also genuinely interested in understanding what the other person is thinking, feeling, wanting or what the message means, and we are active in checking out our understanding before we respond with our own new message. We restate or paraphrase our understanding of their message and reflect it back to the sender for verification. This verification or feedback process is what distinguishes active listening and makes it effective.

Listening effectively can be difficult, because people vary in their communication skills and in how clearly they express themselves and often have different needs, wants and purposes for interacting.

The first step to effective listening is to give yourself permission to really listen to someone. Tell yourself that you are going to focus on what they have to say and give them 100% attention. It also helps if we demonstrate that we are listening and, in face-to-face conversation, eye contact is key.

Really taking an interest in what others have to say will help you to understand people better and to be more empathetic. Everyone has an interesting story to tell and, by actively listening, you will learn so much more about others which will help you to grow and develop as an individual. Not only will you benefit from listening; you will also make other people feel special because listening is the silent form of flattery.

> *Listen or thy tongue will keep thee deaf*

Indian Proverb

Recommended Reading on Listening

Active Listening: Improve Your Ability to Listen and Lead (J-B CCL (Center for Creative Leadership)) by Center for Creative Leadership and Michael H. Hoppe

Listening: A Self-Teaching Guide (Wiley Self-Teaching Guides) by Madelyn Burley-Allen

Listening Skills (Management Shapers) by Ian MacKay

Effective Listening Skills (Business Skills Express Series) by Art James and Dennis Kratz

Visit www.liggywebb.com/hh for additional resources.

Listening Skills - Useful Tips

✓ Give yourself permission to listen and give 100%

✓ Use eye contact and listening body language

✓ Make active listining sounds if you are on the telephone

✓ Be empathic and non-judgmental

✓ Paraphrase and use your own words to check understanding

✓ Don't wait for the gap to jump in with your point

✓ Inhibit your impulse to immediately answer questions

✓ Don't finish peoples sentences

✓ Two ears - one mouth - in that order!

✓ Listen and Learn

Personal Notes & Resolutions

Mental Health

That's the thing about depression: a human being can survive almost anything, as long as she sees the end in sight. But depression is so insidious, and it compounds daily, that it's impossible to ever see the end. The fog is like a cage without a key

Elizabeth Wurtzel

Mental health properly describes a sense of well-being, the capacity to live in a resourceful and fulfilling way and having the resilience to deal with the challenges and obstacles which life presents. Mental health problems or difficulties are terms that can be used to describe temporary reactions to a painful event, stress or external pressures, or systems of drug or alcohol use, lack of sleep or physical illness; this terminology may also be used to describe long-term psychiatric conditions which may have significant effects on an individual's ability to function.

Some of the more common mental health issues include anxiety, depression, mania, paranoia, schizophrenia, eating disorders and obsessive compulsive disorders.

On 9th October 2008, The World Health Organization launched its action programme, the mental health Gap Action Programme (mhGAP), in Geneva, aiming to scale up services for mental, neurological and substance use disorders.

Depression is now set to emerge as the second biggest global health concern after cardiovascular diseases by 2020 and one in four people will be affected by this at least once in their lives. This means that all of us in one way will be directly or indirectly affected.

Currently there is no blood test or brain scan to identify depression so, unlike other physical ailments, its lack of transparency makes it so much more difficult for everyone to deal with. Doctors have to make a diagnosis based on the severity of the patients symptoms; loved ones try to be as supportive as they can whilst feeling frustrated and inadequate; and, for the individual who is suffering with nothing tangible to show, they are left feeling like the invisible patient.

Many factors are involved in depression, which makes it all the more challenging and complex to cope with. A range of factors can be attributed to the illness including genetics, personality traits, attitude, diet, life styles and life events.

It is, however, now a recognised medical fact that depression is usually the result of low levels of the neurotransmitters serotonin, norepinephrine and dopamine – these are all responsible for feelings such as enthusiasm, happiness and gratification.

It is also likely that any abnormalities in various parts of our brain such as the cerebral cortex, hypothalamus and pituitary glands can be responsible for negative thoughts and feelings.

Depression shows itself in many different ways. People don't always realise what's going on because their problems seem to be physical, not mental. They tell themselves they're simply under the weather or feeling tired.

The very nature of depression, which brings a sense of helplessness and worthlessness, can prevent someone who is depressed from seeking help. They often withdraw from friends and relatives around them, rather than asking for help or support. However, this is a time when they need your help and support most. Perhaps the most important thing that you can do is to encourage your friend or relative to seek appropriate treatment.

Try not to blame them for being depressed, or tell them to "pull themselves together". They are probably already blaming themselves, and criticism is likely to make them feel even more depressed. Praise is much more effective than criticism. You can reassure them that it is possible to do something to improve their situation, but you need to do so in a caring and sympathetic way.

Supporting a friend or relative who is depressed can be an opportunity to build a closer and more satisfying relationship. However, it can also be hard work and frustrating, at times. Unless you pay attention to your own needs, it can make you feel depressed, too. Try and share the responsibility with as many people as possible, and find people to whom you can express your frustrations. There may be a local support group of others in your situation.

NB: It is really important that you talk to your GP or another healthcare professional about getting help for yourself and your family.

"It's snowing still," said Eeyore gloomily.
"So it is."
"And freezing."
"Is it?"
"Yes," said Eeyore. "However," he said,
brightening up a little, "we haven't had an
earthquake lately."

A. A. Milne
From the book *Winnie the Pooh*

Recommended Reading on Mental Health

Little Ways to Keep Calm and Carry on: Twenty Lessons for Managing Worry, Anxiety, and Fear by Mark A. Reinecke

A Self-Help Guide to Managing Depression (C & H) by Professor Philip J Barker

Women and Anxiety: A Step-by-step Program for Managing Anxiety and Depression by Helen DeRosis

Managing Severe Depression by Jan Winster

Overcoming Depression: A guide to recovery with a complete self-help programme by Prof Paul Gilbert

Overcoming Anxiety by Helen Kennerley

Free Yourself from Anxiety: A Self-help Guide to Overcoming Anxiety Disorders by Emma Fletcher and Martha Langley

SOS Help for Emotions: Managing Anxiety, Anger, and Depression by Lynn Clark

NB: Please explore the websites at the end of this book to seek further help and advice

Visit www.liggywebb.com/hh for additional resources.

Mental Health - Useful Tips

✓ Wake up with an attitude of gratitude and focus on the positives

✓ Get up half an hour earlier than you would and go for a brisk walk!

✓ Investigate any kind of CBT (Cognitive Behavioural Therapy)

✓ Use positive visualisation techniques

✓ Reduce alcohol - it is a depressive

✓ Build in relaxation and meditative exercises

✓ Exercise 30 minutes every day – this is as good as a mild anti-depressant

✓ Take a Vitamin B Complex – this is great for the nervous system

✓ Keep a thought diary – offload how you feel constructively before you sleep

✓ Remember – you are not alone & try to keep a balanced perspective

Personal Notes & Resolutions

Positive Thinking

*A pessimist sees the difficulty in every opportunity;
an optimist sees the opportunity in every difficulty*

Winston Churchill

Positive thinking is the key to happiness and health and pretty much dictates the way we go about our work and live our lives in general.

A positive attitude is not about a magical mystical mindset possessed by the lucky few. It is something that everyone is capable of achieving and is simply an inclination or leaning toward the positive aspects of any given situation. Thinking positively is not about putting your head in the sand; nor is it about being unrealistic. A positive attitude recognises the negative aspects of a situation, yet chooses to focus instead on the hope and opportunity available. This releases you from getting locked in a paralysing loop of bad feeling and allows you to move quickly to take action and solve difficulties.

Positive thinking and optimism are now known to be a root cause of many life benefits. The relatively new science of *psychoneuroimmunology* looks at how our mind can influence our immune system. The theory is that you will live longer and be healthier and happier by cultivating a positive attitude toward life. In addition, you're more likely to be successful, maintain better relationships and have a beneficial influence on those around you.

Your mental approach to life is a combination of your thoughts, emotions and beliefs. Becoming aware of your emotions, identifying and analysing your thoughts and understanding your beliefs is key to really being able to tackle how you deal with what comes your way.

It is not necessarily what happens to you in life; it is how you react to it.

The most basic indicators of your positivity or negativity are your emotions, which are essentially components of a mental state that arises spontaneously rather than through conscious effort, and are often accompanied by physiological changes.

Creating and maintaining a positive attitude is the most efficient and low-cost investment you can make in order to improve your life. A positive way of thinking is a habit that must be learned through repetition and conscious effort on your part.

A positive attitude is not dependent upon your genetic composition even if you are pre-disposed to negative thinking you can learn to move your thinking to the positive side.

This depends upon how you *choose* to think.

We are faced with literally millions of challenging situations throughout our personal and professional lives. By accepting the reality that we will be faced with many challenges, to which we must seek solutions, it becomes obvious that creating and maintaining a positive attitude can only help us. Our problems remain the same size; it does not matter if you react with bitterness or enthusiasm, and it doesn't change the problem.

Some behavioural psychologists believe that we are like acorns and inside each tiny acorn there is the potential to grow a beautiful oak tree. Many people, who don't break out of their acorn shell, will never have the opportunity to spread their branches and feel the splendour of growth and altitude.

Excuse-making may help us to remain in our comfort zone and negate responsibility, however it is responsibility that separates man from the rest of the animal kingdom. Unlike other animals, we are responsible not for what we have, but for what we could have; not for what we are, but for what we could become. If we are to take credit for our successes, we must assume responsibility for our failures. Excuses are harmful because they prevent us from succeeding. When we make excuses and repeat them often enough, they become a belief. The belief then becomes a self-fulfilling prophecy.

Just look at Thomas Edison, one of the most prolific inventors in history; how many attempts did he have trying to invent the light bulb? As the history books reveal: over 10,000 attempts! He saw possibility and potential where others would have seen limitation and failure.

Positive thinking brings so many benefits to us and truly helps us to explore and discover our true potential. How exciting is that?

> *Become a possibilitarian. No matter how dark things seem to be or actually are, raise your sights and see possibilities – always see them, for they're always there*

Norman Vincent Peale

Recommended Reading on Positive Thinking

The Power of Positive Thinking by Norman Vincent Peale

Everyday Positive Thinking by Louise L. Hay

The Promised Land: A Guide to Positive Thinking for Sufferers of Stress, Anxiety, and Depression by Dr. Rick Norris

Positive Thinking (Essential Managers) by Susan Quilliam

The Book of Positive Quotations for Our Golden Years by Pat Corrick Hinton

Visit www.liggywebb.com/hh for additional resources.

Positive Thinking - Useful Tips

✓ Declare your intent to think positively and be positive

✓ Write down your intention in strong, clear and direct language

✓ Use positive affirmations to condition your mind

✓ Read inspiring books and listen to audio tapes on the subject

✓ At the end of each day, reflect on the positive aspects of the day

✓ Become very aware of your thinking and internal voice

✓ Before going to sleep, reflect upon what you're looking forward to the next day

✓ Write down any concerns you have and challenge them with a positive outcome

✓ Use positive language and challenge your doubts and excuses

✓ Seek out possibilities where others see limitations

Personal Notes & Resolutions

Problem Solving

If you only have a hammer,
you tend to see every problem as a nail

Abraham Maslow

A problem can be a real break and a stroke of luck. It can be seen as opportunity knocking providing you with a chance to get out of the rut of the everyday and make yourself or some situation better. Problems need not arrive as a result of external factors or bad events. Any new awareness you have that allows you to see possibilities for improvement brings a "problem" for you to solve. This is why the most creative people are "problem seekers" rather than "problem avoiders". How you view problem solving is simply a matter of choice.

Developing a positive attitude toward problems can transform you into a happier, saner, more confident person who feels (and is) much more in control of life. You can learn to respond to problems with enthusiasm and eagerness, rising to the opportunity to show your stuff and amazing yourself with some of the results you can achieve!

Problem solving is an essential life skill. It is also a very useful tool because it can help you tackle immediate challenges or achieve a goal. It is a skill because once you have learnt it you can use it repeatedly.

There are a variety of problem solving processes however each process consists of a series of steps, including identifying an issue, searching for options and putting a possible solution into action. It is useful to view problem solving as a cycle because, sometimes, a problem needs several attempts to solve it, or the problem changes.

The first step you need to take is to identify and name the problem so that you can find an appropriate solution. Sometimes you might be unsure about what the problem is: you might just feel general anxiety or be confused about what is getting in the way of your goals.

When you are clear about what the problem is you need to think about it in different ways. Seeing the problem in different ways is likely to help you find an effective solution. This is where creativity can help and the information that we have already covered on this will be useful.

Once you have thought about the problem from different angles, you can identify your goals. What is it that you want to achieve? When you have decided what your goal is, you need to look for possible solutions. The more possible solutions you find, the more likely it is that you will be able to discover an effective solution.

From the list of possible solutions, you can sort out which are most relevant to your situation and which are realistic and manageable. You can do this by predicting outcomes for possible solutions and also checking, with other people, what they think the outcomes might be. When you have explored the consequences, you can use this information to identify the solution which is most relevant to you and is likely to have the best outcomes for your situation.

Once you have selected a possible solution you are ready to put it into action. You will need to have energy and motivation to do this because implementing the solution may take some time and effort. You can prepare yourself to implement the solution by planning when and how you will do it, whether you talk with others about it, and what rewards you will give yourself when you have done it.

Just because you have worked your way through the problem solving process, it does not mean that, by implementing the possible solution, you automatically solve your problem. This where having an alternative back up plan is useful.

If the solution was successful in helping you solve your problem and reaching your goal, then you know that you have effectively solved your problem. If you feel dissatisfied with the result, then you can begin the steps again.

Problem solving is a skill and a process which you can learn, and practice will not only improve your ability; it will help you to gather a whole raft of experience that may help you to solve other problems.

The words problem and opportunity form the hybrid word probortunity. Seeing problems like this and having a positive mental attitude will help you see a way around the rocks in the road as opposed to seeing problems as barriers or obstacles.

> *Problems are only opportunities*
> *with thorns on them*

Hugh Miller

Recommended Reading on Problem Solving

Problem Solving 101: A simple book for smart people: A Simple Guide for Smart People by Ken Watanabe

Decision Making and Problem Solving Strategies - Creating Success series: 66 by John Adair

101 Creative Problem Solving Techniques: The Handbook of New Ideas for Business by James M. Higgins

Problem Solving by Ian S. Robertson

Visit www.liggywebb.com/hh for additional resources.

Problem Solving - Useful Tips

✓ Identify and name your problem

✓ View problems objectively

✓ Look at problems from all angles

✓ Work out what your goal is

✓ Identify alternative solutions

✓ Think creatively

✓ Put the solution into action

✓ Prepare a contingency solution

✓ Review your problem solving process

✓ Be positive and seek out probortunities!

Personal Notes & Resolutions

Relationship Building

The most important single ingredient in the formula of success is knowing how to get along with people

Theodore Roosevelt

One of the most profound experiences that we can have in our lives is the connection we have with other human beings. People in supportive, loving relationships are more likely to feel healthier, happier and more satisfied with their lives and less likely to have mental or physical health problems or to do things that are bad for their health. People in supportive, loving relationships help each other practically as well as emotionally. Supportive partners share the good times and help each other through the tough ones.

A loving friendship can halve the troubles and double the joys and, by doing so, can make life's journey all the more enjoyable. So, when relationships work well, it can be a joyful and positive experience. However, as I am sure we have all experienced, when relationships break down and we find ourselves in a conflict situation or we simply do not connect with someone, it can be draining and disappointing and have a detrimental effect on our self-esteem.

One of the greatest celebrations in life is that we are all different. However, one of the biggest challenges we experience in relationships is that we are all different. We can perceive the world in many ways. Personality profiling indicates how diverse peoples' personalities are and, unlike behaviours, personalities tend to be pretty fixed. We can, however, make choices about the way that we behave around other people.

One of the stumbling blocks that we come across when we try to build relationships is a desire or an expectation that people will think like we do and, in this way, it is so much easier to create a rapport. We feel more comfortable when we feel that people "get" us and can see our point of view. Life, however, would be very dull if we were all the same and, whilst we may find it initially easier, the novelty of sameness would soon wear off.

So, whilst we may have different personalities, the first step to building relationships is to accept that we are all different. We will all have our own unique set of strengths and limitations. It is indeed better and more productive to spend more time concentrating on improving our own limitations than criticising those of others. It would be much more positive to focus on peoples' strengths and accept that, for every strength they have, there is bound to be a perceived weakness. Also, it is important to recognise that sometimes, what we don't like in others is something that we don't like in ourselves!

Certainly, comparing yourself to others is a pointless exercise as we will always find people who are worse or better off than us which in turn will only promote two emotions: one is vanity; the other is bitterness. Neither is a good look!

Focusing on peoples' better qualities and celebrating and feeding back their strengths is a way to reinforce future positive behaviour. Many relationships break down because more time is spent eroding each other's self-esteem through negative criticism and trying to get each other to shrink fit into something or somebody that they are not.

Listening (as we have already established) is a hugely important skill in boosting another person's self-esteem, the silent form of flattery that makes people feel supported and valued. Empathy too is a way of truly connecting with another person by being able to put yourself in their shoes and see their point of view.

Giving time to people is also a huge gift. In a world where time is of the essence and we are trying to fit in more than one lifetime, we don't always have the time to give to our loved ones, friends and work colleagues. Technology has somewhat eroded our ability to build real rapport and we attempt to multi-task by texting and talking at the same time!

Being present in the time you give to people is also very important, so that, when you are with someone, you are truly with someone and not dwelling in the past or worrying about the future.

The connection we make with other people is the very touchstone of our existence and devoting time, energy and effort into developing and building relationships is one of the most valuable life skills.

> *The most important ingredient we put into any relationship is not what we say or what we do, but what we are*

Stephen R. Covey

Recommended Reading on Building Relationships

Relationship Breakthrough: How to create outstanding relationships in every area of your life by Cloe Madanes

Real Small Groups Don't Just Happen: Nurturing Relationships in Your Small Group by Neal F. McBride

Mentoring for Social Inclusion: A Critical Approach to Nurturing Mentor Relationships by Helen Colley

Authentic Relationships: Discover the Lost Art of One Anothering by Wayne Jacobsen and Clay Jacobsen

Visit www.liggywebb.com/hh for additional resources.

Building Relationships - Useful Tips

✓ The relationship you have with yourself is the most important

✓ Actively listen to what other people have to say

✓ Adapt your behaviour to create rapport

✓ Focus on peoples' strengths and give positive feedback

✓ Be constructive with any feedback that may be perceived as negative

✓ Be empathetic and put yourself in others' shoes

✓ Do not punish others for your own insecurities

✓ Be present when you are with people

✓ Invest time and make an effort

✓ Treat people as you would like to be treated yourself

Personal Notes & Resolutions

Relaxation Techniques

Take rest; a field that has rested gives a bountiful crop

Ovid

Building relaxation time into our lives is so important as it can help to keep our stress levels down, and consequently improves our health. Too much work and not enough time out for ourselves can result in physical and mental health problems. So, it's important everybody takes at least ten minutes a day to wind down, whether its soaking in a lovely bubble bath or doing a quick relaxation session before going to sleep or simply listening to some relaxing music.

There are so many wonderful ways you can relax including meditation, massage and yoga. Relaxation is the key when it comes to stress relief therapies. Studies have shown evidence of many other benefits coming from regular relaxation treatments, such as a decrease in the risk of heart attack, protection from mental health problems, improvement of your immune system and your memory. Stress levels are so much higher than they used to be, so it's important for our health to bring these levels down. Sometimes, finding time for ourselves can be difficult so, with added stresses and little spare time, our levels of stress hormones can be raised. This then causes anxiety. Too much adrenaline and cortisol in our bodies can cause our blood pressure to rise, making our brains behave differently.

Sleepless nights can be terrible if your mind's buzzing with information and you desperately need sleep. Relaxation can help you switch off, and you'll be asleep within seconds.

Many people find it difficult to actually relax. Whether it's not having the time to, or finding your mind wanders when trying to relax, it can be difficult, especially if you're a generally busy person.

A lovely hot bubble bath can work wonders. Warm water loosens up muscles, so it's a great way to feel pampered without really doing a lot. It will also deepen respiration and take any tension away from your body, pushing those stresses and strains straight down the plughole! Just a 30 minute soak in a warm bubble bath will help you feel relax and lighten your mind. A hot bath (preferably no hotter than 37° C) can ease tension and make you feel relaxed before going to bed.

Music is a great way of helping you to relax, relive stress and any anxieties you may have. It also helps you function mentally and physically, which is why music is a great therapy. It's regularly used for meditation and Tai Chi, and as an aid for sleep disorders. Studies have suggested that slow, gentle, soothing music can improve learning, creativity and memory. Pachelbel's *Canon in D minor* is wonderful!

Breathing has to be the easiest form of relaxation. This involves inhaling slowly and deeply, counting four seconds in your mind. Hold your breath for another four seconds, then exhale slowly. Feel yourself relaxing as you do this. Feel your shoulders and back sink into the floor as you exhale. Repeat this exercise ten times. After this, breathe normally, but focus on relaxing phrases. Repeat the concentrated breathing exercise another ten times, then breathe normally again. This time focus on pleasurable feelings in your body. Repeat the whole procedure, alternating the inhale-hold-exhale exercise ten times with mental encouragement.

Another technique is something called "Mindfulness". This refers to being completely in touch with and aware of the present moment, as well as taking a non-evaluative and non-judgmental approach to your inner experience. For example, a mindful approach to one's inner experience is simply viewing "thoughts as thoughts" as opposed to evaluating certain thoughts as positive or negative.

The term comes from Eastern spiritual and religious traditions like Zen Buddhism. However, mental health professionals are beginning to recognise that mindfulness can have many benefits for people suffering from difficulties such as anxiety and depression.

The benefits of building relaxation into your day are multiple and chilling out is a way to not only look after yourself physically, mentally and emotionally, it is also the best way to soothe the soul.

There is more to life than increasing its speed

Gandhi

Recommended Reading on Relaxation

Relaxation and Stress Reduction Workbook (New Harbinger Self-Help Workbook) by Martha Davis and Elizabeth Robbins Eshelman

The Fine Arts of Relaxation, Concentration and Meditation: Ancient Skills for Modern Minds by Joel Levey and Michelle Levey

Teach Yourself Relaxation: Relaxation: Alice muir (Teach Yourself - General) by Alice Muir

Relaxation: Exercises and Inspirations for Well-being (Live Better) by Sarah Brewer

Visit www.liggywebb.com/hh for additional resources.

Relaxation - Useful Tips

✓ Get yourself into a comfortable position with no distractions

✓ Adopt a passive attitude and let yourself become relaxed

✓ Concentrate on how you feel and visualise a relaxing image

✓ Think about a one- or two-syllable word to repeat over in your mind, and close your eyes

✓ Relax all of your muscles, starting with your feet and working up the body

✓ Focus on your breathing. Breath in four counts, hold for four counts, exhale ten counts

✓ Imagine worries as balloons and let them go and watch them float away

✓ Have a hot bath with candles and a cup of camomile tea

✓ Listen to classical music – focus on all the instruments and notes

✓ Build in time every day to relax

Personal Notes & Resolutions

Self Awareness

Knowing others is wisdom;
knowing yourself is enlightenment

Lao Tzu

Self-awareness is a recognition of our personality, our strengths and weaknesses, our likes and dislikes. Developing self-awareness can help us to recognise when we are stressed or under pressure. It is also often a prerequisite for effective communication and interpersonal relations, as well as for developing empathy for others.

Self-awareness is the first step in the creation process. As you grow in self-awareness, you will better understand why you feel what you feel and why you behave as you behave. That understanding then gives you the opportunity and freedom to change those things you'd like to change about yourself and create the life you want. Without fully knowing who you are, self-acceptance and change become impossible

One of the keys to becoming more self aware is to know yourself better and also be able to show yourself with less inhibition. If you know yourself well enough, you will have the confidence to be more open and share relevant information to improve communication and connect better with others.

One tool to help you with this is the *Johari Window,* a model named after the first names of its inventors, Joseph Loft and Harry Ingham in 1955. It is one of the most useful models describing the process of human interaction. Based on a four-paned "window", it divides personal awareness into four different types, as represented by its four quadrants: open, hidden, blind, and unknown.

We have to begin with an "open" pane which is our "arena" which is what you know about yourself and so do others. Our second "closed" pane is our "façade" which is what others don't know about us, but we do know about ourselves. Essentially it's your secrets, the things you keep to yourself because you either want to keep them private or you fear letting other people know about them in case they judge or reject you.

Our third "blind" pane is our "blind spot" which is what others know about you, but you don't know about yourself; this could be something obvious like physical behaviours or mannerisms. The final "unknown" pane is our personal potential which is what we don't know about ourselves and neither do others. It is our *Unknown Self* waiting to be discovered. Our potential waiting to be unleashed.

So, in order to understand ourselves better and to feel the confidence to show ourselves more, we need to trust in order to be more open and accept feedback to learn more about ourselves from other perspectives.

Trust is something that requires a certain amount of confidence and also the ability to occasionally move out of our comfort zone. Receiving feedback can also be challenging. It is the food of progress, but, like some foods, while it may be good for us, it can also not be so pleasant to digest. However, the more we can let our guard down and open up, and the more we see feedback as free information that can add huge value, or be dissuaded (it is our choice after all) the more potential we have to grow and see ourselves more clearly in the metaphorical mirror.

Emotional Intelligence - EQ - is a relatively recent behavioural model, rising to prominence with Daniel Goleman's 1995 book called *Emotional Intelligence*. The skill of self-awareness forms a large part of emotional intelligence and, by being more self aware, we are better equipped to understand why we react in certain ways to certain things – which helps us to take more personal responsibility for ourselves on an emotional level.

The more we understand about ourselves, the better equipped we will be to deal with the challenges we face and this, in turn, will boost our self confidence and help us to maximise our personal potential.

> *To have greater self-awareness or understanding means to have a better grasp of reality*

Dalai Lama

Recommended Reading on Self Awareness

Emotional Intelligence by Daniel Goleman

If It Could Happen to Buddha, Why Not You: Understanding the Ancient Secrets of Self Awareness by Dr Vacant Joshi

Self-Awareness: The Hidden Driver of Success and Satisfaction by Travis Brad berry

The Curse of the Self: Self-awareness, egotism, and the quality of human life by Mark R. Leary

Eight Steps to Heaven: A Simple Guide into Self-awareness and Spiritual Development by Glyn Parry

Visit www.liggywebb.com/hh for additional resources.

Self Awareness - Useful Tips

✓ Encourage feedback about your blind spots

✓ Reach out of your comfort zone

✓ Learn to trust more and open up to others

✓ Don't be afraid to make mistakes

✓ Be interested in who you are

✓ Listen to yourself and challenge your insecurities

✓ Identify your personal strengths and weaknesses

✓ Take a psychometric test

✓ Be open to self improvement – nobody is perfect!

✓ Learn to love yourself – warts and all!

Personal Notes & Resolutions

Self-Confidence

A man cannot be comfortable without his own approval

Mark Twain

The real key to self-confidence is about believing in yourself and trusting your own views and opinions. At times, this can be difficult, especially if you have a tendency to listen to others and benchmark yourself against what they think of you. This is, however, very dangerous and the ability to establish your own inner benchmark to success is essential.

Every human being has the ability to take control and make positive changes. Other people can try and stop you, but only if you let them. When you look in the mirror, be proud of the person that you see, knowing that you do the best you can.

Tell yourself that you are confident and believe in yourself. Focus on your strengths and the positive aspects of your character and set about developing the areas that you have for potential.

The way a person carries themselves tells a story. People with slumped shoulders and lethargic movements display a lack of self-confidence. They aren't enthusiastic about what they're doing and they don't consider themselves important. By practising good posture, you'll automatically feel more confident. Stand up straight, keep your head up, and make eye contact. You'll make a positive impression on others and instantly feel more alert and empowered.

One of the best ways to build confidence is listening to a motivational speech. There are some great CDs out there. You can even write your own. Write a 30- to 60-second speech that highlights your strengths and goals. Then recite it in front of the mirror aloud (or inside your head if you prefer) whenever you need a confidence boost.

When we think negatively about ourselves, we often project that feeling on to others in the form of insults and gossip. To break this cycle of negativity, get into the habit of praising other people. Refuse to engage in backstabbing gossip and make an effort to compliment those around you. In the process, you'll become well-liked and, by looking for the best in others, you will, indirectly, bring out the best in yourself.

In meetings and public assemblies around the world, people constantly strive to sit at the back of the room. Most people prefer the back because they're afraid of being noticed. This reflects a lack of self-confidence. By deciding to sit in the front row, you can get over this irrational fear and build your self-confidence. You'll also be more visible to the important people talking from the front of the room.

During group discussions and meetings at work, many people never speak up because they're afraid that people will judge them for saying something stupid. This fear isn't really justified. Generally, people are much more accepting than we imagine. In fact, most people are dealing with the exact same fears. By making an effort to speak up at least once in every group discussion, you'll become a better public speaker, more confident in your own thoughts, and recognised as a leader by your peers.

Along the same lines as personal appearance, physical fitness has a huge effect on self-confidence. If you're out of shape, you'll feel insecure, unattractive, and less energetic. By working out, you improve your physical appearance, energise yourself, and accomplish something positive. Having the discipline to work out not only makes you feel better, it creates positive momentum that you can build on for the rest of the day.

Too often we get caught up in our own desires. We focus too much on ourselves and not enough on the needs of other people. If you stop thinking about yourself and concentrate on the contribution you're making to the rest of the world, you won't worry as much about you own flaws. This will increase self-confidence and allow you to contribute with maximum efficiency. The more you contribute to the world, the more you'll be rewarded with personal success and recognition.

> *Make the most of yourself,*
> *for that is all there is of you*

Ralph Waldo Emerson

Recommended Reading on Self-Confidence

Self-confidence: The Remarkable Truth of Why a Small Change Can Make a Big Difference by Paul McGee

Evolving Self-confidence: How to Become Free from Anxiety Disorders and Depression by Terry Dixon

Building Self-Confidence For Dummies by Kate Burton and Brinley Platts

Instant Confidence by Paul McKenna

Visit www.liggywebb.com/hh for additional resources.

Self Confidence - Useful Tips

✓ Believe in yourself first and foremost

✓ Tell yourself that you feel confident

✓ Develop confident non-verbal communication

✓ Read motivational books and quotes

✓ Be grateful for what you have

✓ Compliment other people

✓ Sit in the front row in meetings

✓ Speak up during meetings and discussions

✓ Exercise and energise and trigger your happy hormones

✓ Walk faster and put a spring in your step

✓ Look upwards and outwards

Personal Notes & Resolutions

Stress Management

Tension is who you think you should be.
Relaxation is who you are

Chinese Proverb

The pressure of modern living is becoming more and more challenging for so many people these days. If real life was like being on the set of a reality TV show – and as easily manipulated – many people, when overwhelmed with the burden of stress, would sooner be voted off!

Clearly, in the real world, we don't have that as an easy option, and being able to develop our personal coping strategy is essential to maintaining our physical and mental health.

The term "stress-related burn-out" is becoming commonplace, especially in the workplace where many people spend the majority of their waking hours. Of course, what is stressful for one person may not be stressful for another. We all react differently, with some people thriving on it while others crumble.

The interesting thing is that no one really knew that they were "stressed" until around 1956. The word "stress" was not included in our vocabulary until Hans Seyle, a Canadian physician and endocrinologist, defined it over fifty years ago. His pioneering work into the influence of stress on people's ability to cope with and adapt to pressure has opened a fascinating debate into the pros and cons of this modern-day phenomenon. His belief was that it isn't stress that can kill us; it is our reaction to it. And, by adopting the right attitude, we can convert a negative reaction to stress into a positive one.

Stress, despite the dangers, does also bring some benefits. We all need a certain amount of pressure in our lives to galvanise us into action and "healthy stress" can be productive and act as a motivator. However, too much pressure or prolonged pressure can lead to stress disorders, which are unhealthy for the mind and body.

Anxiety and depression are some of the most common mental health problems and the majority of cases are caused by stress. Research by mental health charity MIND also suggests that a quarter of the population will have a mental health problem at some point in their lives.

When faced with a situation that makes you stressed, your body releases chemicals, including cortisol, adrenaline and noradrenalin. These invoke the "fight or flight" feelings that help us to deal with the situation. However, when you're in a situation that prevents you from fighting or escaping, such as being on an overcrowded train, these chemicals are not used.

If the chemicals that are released during stressful situations accumulate from not being used, their effects are felt by the body. A build-up of adrenaline and noradrenalin increases blood pressure, heart rate, and the amount that you sweat. Cortisol prevents your immune system from functioning properly, as well as releasing fat and sugar into your blood stream.

Stress is a well-known trigger for depression and it can also affect your physical health. So it's important to identify the causes of stress in your life and try to minimise them.

Any sort of loss, from bereavement, divorce and separation to a child leaving home, causes stress, as do long-term illness and disability. But things such as marriage, moving house, a new job and holidays have quite high stress ratings too.

In work, worrying about deadlines or about not being up to the challenges of a particular task can cause stress.

Every one of us is unique in the way that we respond to stress. However, some common signs may include: increased irritability, heightened sensitivity, signs of tension (such as nail-biting), difficulty getting to sleep and waking up in the morning, drinking and smoking more, loss of appetite or comfort eating, loss of concentration and lack of emotional control.

If you suffer from any of these, it is so important to take action to relieve damaging stress before it affects your physical or mental health.

The secret of managing stress is to look after yourself and, where possible, remove some of the causes of stress. If you start to feel things are getting on top of you, then do something about it straight away.

> *A crust eaten in peace is better than*
> *a banquet partaken in anxiety*

Aesop, *Fables*

Recommended Reading on Stress Management

Stress Management for Dummies by Allen Elkin

Meditation - The Stress Solution by Mary Pearson

Stress Management: A Comprehensive Guide to Wellness by Edward A. Charlesworth and Ronald G. Nathan

Relaxation and Stress Reduction Workbook (New Harbinger Self-Help Workbook) by Martha Davis and Elizabeth Robbins Eshelman

The Big Book of Stress Relief Games: Quick, Fun Activities for Feeling Better (Big Book Series) by Robert Epstein

Visit www.liggywebb.com/hh for additional resources.

Stress Management - Useful Tips

✓ Exercise is one of the very best ways to reduce stress

✓ Breathing exercises will reduce stress immediately

✓ Avoid caffeinated drinks and alcohol

✓ Focus on simplicity and do one thing at a time

✓ Know your own limits; don't expect too much of yourself

✓ Talk to someone and discuss constructive ways to deal with stress

✓ Study and learn time-management techniques

✓ Try to spend time with people who are positive

✓ Use visualisation techniques

✓ Explore alternative therapies

Personal Notes & Resolutions

Time Management

But what minutes! Count them by sensation, and not by calendars, and each moment is a day

Benjamin Disraeli

Imagine if time was a bank account and, each morning, you were credited with 86,400 seconds. If, by the end of that day you hadn't spent any of the credits they would instantly be deducted from your account. What would you do?

Well the chances are, I expect, that you would make every effort to spend them. It's amazing, isn't it, how much we take time for granted and then regret the moments we lost?

In transport economics, the value of time is the opportunity cost of the time that a traveller spends on their journey. In essence, this makes it the amount that a traveller would be willing to pay in order to save time, or the amount they would accept as compensation for lost time. The value of time varies considerably from person to person and depends upon the purpose of the journey, but can generally be divided into two sets of valuations: working time and non-working time.

One of the biggest challenges that many people face is personal time management and the ability to prioritise.

Let's face it; we all have our own quirky little habits that we have adopted and I am sure we have all been guilty of putting ourselves and other people under unnecessary pressure by just not being as well-organised as we could.

It is important to respect other peoples' time and, if our own lack of personal organisation or timekeeping disrupts others, then it is important that we take responsibility and do something about it.

Also, it is worth considering that, no matter how organised we may be, there are always only 24 hours in a day. Time doesn't change. All we can actually manage is ourselves and what we do with the time that we have. Many of us are prey to time-wasters that steal time we could be using much more productively. It is so easy to go off-track or become distracted by something that is so much more interesting than the task in hand.

Procrastination is the ultimate thief of time, and putting off what we can do today is something many people are guilty of. It is actually far better to do the thing you least like doing first so that it doesn't hang over you making you feel gloomy at the prospect.

It is important to remember, the focus of time management is actually changing your behaviours, not changing time. A good place to start is by eliminating your personal time-wasters. For one week, for example, set a goal that you are going to change one time-wasting habit that you are aware of.

Think of this as an extension of time management . The objective is to change your behaviours over time to achieve whatever general goal you've set for yourself, such as increasing your productivity or decreasing your stress. So you need to not only set your specific goals, but track them over time to see whether or not you're accomplishing them.

A good suggestion is to start each day with a time management session prioritising the tasks for that day and setting yourself a performance benchmark. If you have twenty tasks for a given day, how many of them do you truly need to accomplish? Put them into two categories, essential and non-essential, and make sure you do the essential tasks first even if they are the ones you don't necessarily enjoy the most.

Rewarding yourself and setting yourself little treats is a good way to motivate yourself, even if it is just taking a five minute break to recharge your batteries before you set about your next task!

The key benefit of time management is that it will free up precious time, reduce your stress levels and boost your self-esteem as you manage yourself more effectively and efficiently. Time is precious; don't waste a moment!

> *Yesterday is history*
>
> *Tomorrow is a mystery*
>
> *Today is a gift*
>
> *That's why it's called the present*

Recommended Reading on Time Management

Time Management for Dummies (UK Edition) by Clare Evans

Do it Tomorrow and Other Secrets of Time Management by Mark Forster

The 25 Best Time Management Tools and Techniques: How to Get More Done without Driving Yourself Crazy by Pamela Dodd and Doug Sundheim

How to Be Organized in Spite of Yourself: Time and Space Management That Works with Your Personal Style (How to Be) by Sunny Schlenger and Roberta Roesch

Visit www.liggywebb.com/hh for additional resources.

Time Management - Useful Tips

✓ Accept that there are only 24 hours in a day!

✓ Find out where you're wasting time

✓ Create time management goals

✓ Implement a time management plan

✓ Use time management tools

✓ Prioritise ruthlessly and confidently

✓ Learn to delegate and outsource when you can

✓ Establish routines and stick to them as much as possible

✓ Get in the habit of setting time limits for tasks

✓ Make sure your systems are well organised

Personal Notes & Resolutions

Work-Home Balance

*Work, love and play are the great
balance wheels of man's being*

Orison Swett Marde

Work-Life Balance is a phrase that has been bandied
about since the 1970s. Personally, I think the term
Work-Home balance is a better description. Work-Life
balance tends to infer that we go to work and we have
a life! The reality is that many of us spend more time at
work than we do at home and more time with our work
colleagues than we do with our friends and family so it
is a huge part of our lives.

Work is fast becoming the way in which we define
ourselves. It is now answering some of the traditional
questions like "Who am I?" and "How do I find meaning
and purpose in my life?" Work is no longer just about
economics; it's about identity. About fifty years ago,
people had many sources of identity: religion, class,
nationality, political affiliation, family roots, geo-
graphical and cultural origins and more. Today, many of
these, if not all, have been superseded by work.

Over the past thirty years, there has been a substantial
increase in workload which is felt to be due, in part, to
the use of information technology and to an intense,
competitive work environment.

Long-term loyalty and a sense of corporate community have been eroded by a performance culture that expects more and more from employees yet offers little support in return.

Many experts forecasted that technology would eliminate most household chores and provide people with much more time to enjoy leisure activities. Unfortunately, many have decided to ignore this option, being egged on by a consumerist culture and a political agenda that has elevated the work ethic to unprecedented heights.

An alarming amount of absenteeism in the workplace is now stress-related and it is clear that problems caused by stress have become a major concern to both employers and employees. Symptoms are manifested both physiologically and psychologically. Persistent stress can result in a range of problems, including frequent headaches, stiff muscles and backache. It can also result in irritability, insecurity, exhaustion and difficulty concentrating.

It is now more important than ever that people learn to manage their work life and home life so that they create a better balance that reduces stress and promotes better long-term health.

The idea of work/home balance is further complicated by the fact that today's workforce is more culturally diverse and also made up of different generations, each with its own set of priorities. Additionally, businesses are in various stages of their own life cycles. Instead of looking for a generic, standardised concept of work/home balance, we need to understand that it is our own responsibility to make sure that we implement personal strategies that help us to get a better perspective on how we balance our time and energy between the two.

One important thing is the distinction between work and home – and to be aware of the negativities that we can potentially carry between the two. If we are not careful, it can become a bad habit that, at the end of a each busy day, we offload to our partners all our moans and whinges about our work day, thus infecting our home lives with the stress of work. A good habit to get into is spend time at the end of each day sharing your achievements and successes and focusing on the positive outcomes of the day.

Work and home life are equally important, and the key to happiness is about finding the right balance so you can get the best and the most out of both of them

When people go to work, they shouldn't have to leave their hearts at home

Betty Bender

Recommended Reading on Work - Home Balance

How to Work Wonders by Liggy Webb

The See-saw: 100 Ideas for Work-life Balance: 100 Recipes for Work-life Balance by Julia Hobsbawm

The One Minute Manager Balances Work and Life by Ken Blanchard, D. W. Edington, and Marjorie Blanchard

Harvard Business Review on Work and Life Balance ("Harvard Business Review" Paperback) by Harvard Business Review

Work-life Balance for Dummies by Jeni Mumford and Katherine Lockett

Visit www.liggywebb.com/hh for additional resources.

Work-Home Balance - Useful Tips

✓ Schedule brief breaks for yourself throughout the day

✓ At the end of each day, set your priorities for the following day

✓ Make a distinction between work and the rest of your life

✓ Address concerns about deadlines and deliverables early

✓ Make sure you take all of your allocated holidays

✓ Create a buffer between work and home

✓ Decide what chores can be shared or let go

✓ Make time for exercise and relaxation

✓ When you get home, focus on positive outcomes from the day

✓ Pursue a hobby that has nothing to do with your work

Personal Notes & Resolutions

Happy Stuff

Happy Quotations

There are some wonderful quotations about happiness that can provoke so much positive thought. Here is a compilation of some wonderful pearls of wisdom ...

Happiness is having a sense of self - not a feeling of being perfect but of being good enough and knowing that you are in the process of growth, of being, of achieving levels of joy. It's a wonderful contentment and acceptance of who and what you are and a knowledge that the world and the life are full of wondrous adventures and possibilities, and you are part of the centre. It's an awareness that no matter what happens you will somehow be able to deal with it, knowing that everything does pass and even your deepest despair will vanish

Leo. F. Buscaglia

This above all, to thine own self be true

William Shakespeare

Rich people constantly learn and grow. Poor people think they already know

T. Harv Eker

Whoever said money can't buy happiness didn't know where to shop

Gertrude Stein

Some cause happiness wherever they go; others, whenever they go

Oscar Wilde

Happiness is good health and a bad memory

Ingrid Bergman

It is pretty hard to tell what does bring happiness; poverty and wealth have both failed

Kin Hubbard

If there were in the world today any large number of people who desired their own happiness more than they desired the unhappiness of others, we could have paradise in a few years

Bertrand Russell

The good life, as I conceive it, is a happy life. I do not mean that if you are good you will be happy – I mean that if you are happy you will be good

Bertrand Russell

To be without some of the things you want is an indispensable part of happiness

Bertrand Russell

Men who are unhappy, like men who sleep badly, are always proud of the fact

Bertrand Russell

One should as a rule respect public opinion in so far as is necessary to avoid starvation and to keep out of prison, but anything that goes beyond this is voluntary submission to an unnecessary tyranny, and is likely to interfere with happiness in all kinds of ways

Bertrand Russell

My life has no purpose, no direction, no aim, no meaning, and yet I'm happy. I can't figure it out. What am I doing right?

Charles Schulz

In Hollywood, if you don't have happiness you send out for it

Rex Reed

Happiness: a good bank account, a good cook, and a good digestion

Jean Jacques Rousseau

I am a kind of paranoiac in reverse. I suspect people of plotting to make me happy

J. D. Salinger

A man doesn't know what happiness is until he's married. By then it's too late

Frank Sinatra

The more one is hated, I find, the happier one is

Louis-Ferdinand Destouches

The happy people are failures because they are on such good terms with themselves they don't give a damn

Agatha Christie

Do not dwell in the past, do not dream of the future, concentrate the mind on the present moment

Buddha

All happiness depends on a leisurely breakfast

John Gunther

To laugh often and much;

To win the respect of intelligent people and the affection of children;

To earn the appreciation of honest critics and endure the betrayal of false friends;

To appreciate beauty, to find the best in others;

To leave the world a bit better, whether by a healthy child, a garden patch, or a redeemed social condition;

To know even one life has breathed easier because you have lived.

This is to have succeeded

Ralph Waldo Emerson 1803 – 1882

Although the world is full of suffering … it is also full of overcoming it

Helen Keller

It's only by going down into the abyss
that we recover the treasures of life.
Where you stumble
there lies your treasure.
The very cave you are afraid to enter
turns out to be the source of
what you were looking for

Joseph Campbell

It does not matter how slow you go so long as you do
not stop

Confucius

Happiness is the meaning and the purpose of life, the
whole aim and end of human existence

Aristotle

Shared joy is a double joy; shared sorrow is half sorrow

Swedish proverb

Happy Music

Music is a wonderful way to make you feel happy and upbeat – here are a few tracks selected that will lift your spirit.

Build Me Up Buttercup - The Foundations
Chain Reaction - Diana Ross
Daydream Believer - The Monkees
Don't Stop Believin' - Glee Cast
Don't Stop Me Now - Queen
Don't Worry Be Happy - Bobby McFerrin
Flashdance What A Feeling - Irene Cara
Heaven Is A Place On Earth - Belinda Carlisle
Hey, Soul Sister - Train
Hot N Cold - Katy Perry
I Got You Babe - UB40 Featuring Chrissie Hynde
I'll Be There For You (Theme From Friends) - The Rembrandts
I'm Gonna Be (500 Miles) - The Proclaimers
I'm Yours - Jason Mraz
What A Wonderful World - Louis Armstrong
Our House - Madness
Pack Up - Eliza Doolittle
Smile - Lily Allen
The Tide Is High - Blondie
Under The Boardwalk - The Drifters
Walking On Sunshine - Katrina & The Waves
We Are Family - Sister Sledge

Happy Classical Music

- Pachelbel - Canon
- Tchaikovsky - The Nutcracker Suite & Swan Lake
- Strauss - Blue Danube
- Haydn - Menuet from the Surprise Symphony
- Borodin - Polovtsian Dance from "Prince Igor"
- Rossini - Overture from "Barber of Seville"
- Johann Strauss - Polkas
- Sousa - Marches
- Rimsky-Korsakov - Flight of the Bumblebee
- Chopin - Raindrop Prelude
- Ethelbert Nevin - Narcissus
- Peer Gynt - In the Hall of the Mountain King
- Holst - Planets
- Stravinsky - Rite of Spring
- Wagner - Der Ring des Nibelungen
- Rimsky-Korsakov - Scherehzade
- Copland - Appalachian Spring
- Mussorgsky - Pictures at an Exhibition
- Richard Strauss - Death and Transfiguration
- Vivaldi - La Primavera Allegro
- Rossini - William Tell Overture
- Sir Henry Wood - Trumpet Voluntary
- Enrico Mancini - The Pink Panther
- Johann Strauss II - Liebesbotschaft-galopp

Happy Films

The Shawshank Redemption (1994) - Frank Darabont's prison drama "The Shawshank Redemption" is one of the best movies ever made. This film epitomises the power of optimism and has some wonderfully inspiring moments that will provide you with the ultimate feel good factor!

Little Miss Sunshine (2006) - Road movies seem to be a great starting point for happy films. It is after all a journey that the audience and the characters take, discovering humanity and their own humanness along the way. "Little Miss Sunshine" is a vibrant, hopeful, and funny film with some wonderful characters and performances.

Amelie (2001) - "Amelie" is a sugar-coated, rose-tinted story of self-discovery set against the backdrop of a picture-perfect Paris. The city is painted in vibrant hues to encapsulate the romanticism of the place everyone goes to in order to fall in love, or so the film would have you believe.

Forrest Gump (1994) – Life is like a box of chocolates! Robert Zemeckis' film is both sentimental and epic in scope. With a great performance from Tom Hanks and a wonderfully orchestrated whistle-stop tour of American history it will soar your spirit and make you smile.

Planes, Trains, and Automobiles (1987) - Two 1980s comedy greats come together for this endlessly funny road movie about an uptight advertising executive (Steve Martin) and his slobby yet lovable travel-mate (John Candy). With an ending that layers sentiment on sentiment, "Planes, Trains, and Automobiles" makes sure you know you're witnessing a happy conclusion.

Modern Times (1936) - Watching Charlie Chaplin clumsily navigate the huge metallic cogs of a factory machine you are reminded of the marvelous talent of the man as well as a more refined and simple time for Hollywood when everything had to be done by hand. Chaplin was a genius and this is one of his most entertaining films.

It's a Wonderful Life (1946) - Prescribed by psychiatrists as a remedy for their patient's depression, "It's A Wonderful Life" is Hollywood's answer for increasing those serotonin levels. It remains a firm favourite amongst audiences for its life-affirming story and James Stewart's wonderful performance.

Groundhog Day (1993) - One of the funniest comedies of the 1990s, "Groundhog Day" has quickly established itself among audiences as the go-to movie for a quick-fix cheer-up. Bill Murray is brilliant as grumpy weatherman Phil Connors who has to live out the same day over and over again.

Duck Soup (1933) - On its release in 1933 "Duck Soup" wasn't considered as anything special. How opinion has changed. Now it is generally considered a masterpiece and arguably the finest film made by the Marx Brothers.

His Girl Friday (1940) - A screwball comedy in the best sense of the word, Howard Hawks quick-witted "His Girl Friday" sees Cary Grant at the top of his game as Walter Burns, the tough nut editor of The Morning Post. Considered by critics as one of the greatest comedies ever made, Hawks' films is best known for its accelerated dialogue.

Finding Nemo (2003) - Pixar's best film is about a clownfish on an adventure across the ocean to find his son. It's a heart-warming tale of familial loyalty and friendship, set against the backdrop of Pixar's scintillating computer generated ocean.

Some Like It Hot (1959) - This timeless comedy from Billy Wilder is a joy from start to finish. Jack Lemmon and Tony Curtis couldn't be better, while Marilyn Monroe's radiant beauty and seductive charm is enough to make you fall in love with this film over and over again. "Some Like It Hot" also benefits from having one of the best, and funniest, endings ever.

Cinema Paradiso (1988) "Cinema Paradiso" is a richly detailed tale of friendship, largely set in Sicily. Told mainly in flashback we learn of Salvatore's younger, formative years and the bond he made with cinema projectionist Alfredo. There is also a love for cinema that permeates through the film.

Life Is Beautiful (1997)   Roberto Benigni who made this wonderful tale that celebrates the human spirit. It will pull at your heartstrings but "Life Is Beautiful" is all about the vitality of life in the midst of the destructiveness of war. Roger Ebert said it perfectly: "Life Is Beautiful" is not about Nazis and Fascists, but about the human spirit.

The Goodbye Girl (1977) - Richard Dreyfuss and Marsha Mason star as the unlikely couple in Herbert Ross' film based on Neil Simon's screenplay. Dreyfuss and Mason are perfectly cast in a film that benefits from one of Simon's most accomplished scripts. Funny, bittersweet, and loveable.

Harold and Maude (1971) - That director Hal Ashby can make an optimistic film about the death of an old lady and the recurring suicidal tendencies of a confused young man tells you a lot about this film's unique charm. It finds little pieces of joy in the most obscure places that make living all the more worthwhile.

E.T - The Extra-Terrestrial (1982) - Two lost and innocent children – one human, one alien – find friendship and adventure in a Californian suburb. The film might be otherworldly but its message is universally appealing. By the end you'll be weeping with happy tears and going right back to the start for another magical journey.

The Sound of Music (1965) - One of the greatest musicals ever made, Robert Wise's film about carefree nanny Maria (Julie Andrews) instilling fun and frivolity into the lives of the Von Trapp family children is one of the most likable stories ever told on film.

Stand By Me (1986) - Of the Stephen King novellas that have found their way to the big screen this is the best of them. With brilliant performances – the best of which by the late River Phoenix – you can't fail to engage with their sense of adventure, and the bond they forge as they journey along the rail tracks.

The Wizard of Oz (Fleming, USA, 1939) - The wonder of film and sheer spectacle comes through "The Wizard of Oz" like few other movies. Dorothy's adventure along the Yellow Brick Road is one filled with wonderful characters and some of the most memorable songs ever written.

Visit www.liggywebb.com/hh for more "Happy Recommendations".

Useful Websites

www.alcoholconcern.org.uk

Alcohol Concern is the national agency on alcohol misuse campaigning for effective alcohol policy and improved services for people whose lives are affected by alcohol-related problems.

www.backcare.org.uk

BackCare is a national charity that aims to reduce the impact of back pain on society by providing information, support, promoting good practice and funding research. BackCare acts as a hub between patients, (healthcare) professionals, employers, policy makers, researchers and all others with an interest in back pain.

www.bacp.co.uk

British Association for Counselling and Psychotherapy is the largest and broadest body within the sector. Through its work BACP ensures that it meets its remit of public protection whilst also developing and informing its members. Its work with large and small organisations within the sector ranges from advising schools on how to set up a counselling service, assisting the NHS on service provision, working with voluntary agencies and supporting independent practitioners.

BACP participates in the development of counselling and psychotherapy at an international level.

www.bhfactive.org.uk

The British Heart Foundation National Centre for Physical Activity and Health (BHFNC) is committed to developing and promoting initiatives that will help professionals stimulate more people to take more activity as part of everyday life.

www.cipd.co.uk

The Chartered Institute of Personnel and Development (CIPD) is Europe's largest HR and development professional body. With over 135,000 members, they pride themselves on supporting and developing those responsible for the management and development of people within organisations.

www.counsellingatwork.org.uk

BACP Workplace is the home for counsellors in workplace settings and the forum for all professionals with an interest in counselling, employee support and psychological health at work. BACP Workplace promotes professional counselling and the development of employee support in the workplace. As specialist division of the British Association for Counselling and Psychotherapy, BACP Workplace promotes best practice and provides a forum and mutual support network for individuals and organisations working in this area.

www.dh.gov.uk

The Department of Health is committed to improving the quality and convenience of care provided by the NHS and social services. Its work includes setting national standards, shaping the direction of health and social care services and promoting healthier living.

www.drugscope.org.uk

DrugScope is the UK's leading independent centre of information and expertise on drugs and the national membership organisation for the drug field. It aims to inform policy development and reduce drug-related harms – to individuals, families and communities.

www.isma.org.uk

ISMA[UK] is a registered charity with a multi-disciplinary professional membership that includes the UK and the Republic of Ireland. It exists to promote sound knowledge and best practice in the prevention and reduction of human stress. It sets professional standards for the benefit of individuals and organisations using the services of its members.

www.mentalhealth.org.uk

The Mental Health Foundation is a UK charity that provides information, carries out research, campaigns and works to improve services for anyone affected by mental health problems, whatever their age and wherever they live. Their vision is a mentally healthy world where people are free from the suffering caused by mental illness.

www.workplacewellness.org

Workplace Wellness is an innovative employee and family assistance program in the US. In addition to counselling services, Workplace Wellness takes special pride in their commitment to education, training and management consultation. They believe that educated, well-informed employees are the primary ingredients of a healthy and productive workforce. Their goal is to support the wellness of employees, whether at work or home, for the mutual benefit of both the individual and the employer.

www.dietandfitnessresources.co.uk

UK site that sells fitness equipment and diet resoucrses.

www.nhsplus.nhs.uk

NHS Plus serves to increase the quality and delivery of health and work services and supports the broader Health, Work and Wellbeing Strategy through; helping develop the NHS as a model employer, delivering services to other public sector bodies and smaller businesses and supporting the development of quality occupational health practices.

www.workingfamilies.org.uk

Working Families is the UK's leading work-life balance organisation. We help children, working parents and carers and their employers find a better balance between responsibilities at home and work.

www.som.org.uk

The Society of Occupational Medicine is a charity and a forum for its membership and aims to stimulate interest, research and education in Occupational Medicine. It has wide-ranging contacts with government departments and professional bodies and responds with the Society's view to consultative documents and topics of interest and concern affecting the speciality.

www.sportengland.org

Sport England is focused on the creation of a world-leading community sport system in the UK. They invest National Lottery and Exchequer funding in organisations and projects that will grow and sustain participation in grassroots sport and create opportunities for people to excel at their chosen sport.

www.stress.org.uk

The Stress Management Society is a non-profit making organization dedicated to helping people tackle stress. They combine their knowledge of stress and how to tackle it with an impartial view of stress management products and services. They only recommend products or services that they know work.

www.theworkfoundation.com

The Work Foundation is the leading independent authority on work and its future. It aims to improve the quality of working life and the effectiveness of organisations by equipping leaders, policymakers and opinion-formers with evidence, advice, new thinking and networks.

www.workstress.net

The UK National Work-Stress Network is committed to the eradication of the causes of work-related stress and associated illnesses. It campaigns to advance this aim through its involvement with the Hazards Campaign; and in conjunction with the TUC, European organisations, within UK Trades Union structures.

www.workwiseuk.org

Work Wise UK is a not-for-profit initiative, which aims to make the UK one of the most progressive economies in the world by encouraging the widespread adoption of smarter working practices.

An increasingly complex world means that employers and employees have to strive to use their resources effectively; one to gain better productivity, the other to balance work-life pressures.

www.apa.org

American Psychological Association (APA) is a scientific and professional organization that represents psychology in the United States. The mission of the APA is to advance the creation, communication and application of psychological knowledge to benefit society and improve people's lives.

www.nmha.org

Mental Health America is the USA's largest and oldest community-based network dedicated to helping all Americans live mentally healthier lives. With more than 300 affiliates across the country, they touch the lives of millions - Advocating for changes in policy; Educating the public & providing critical information; & delivering urgently needed Programs and Services.

www.depression-screening.org/depression_ screen.cfm

An online depression-screening test is one of the quickest and easiest ways to determine whether you are experiencing symptoms of clinical depression. The depression-screening test on this site is completely anonymous and confidential. The screening test on this web site is intended solely for the purpose of identifying the symptoms of depressive disorders.

www.mentalhealth.com

Internet Mental Health is a free encyclopaedia of mental health information created by a Canadian psychiatrist, Dr. Phillip Long.

www.mentalhelp.net

The Mental Help Net website exists to promote mental health and wellness education and advocacy.

www.liveyourlifewell.org

The America's leading non-profit dedicated to helping ALL people live mentally healthier lives. With more than 320 affiliates nationwide, they represent a growing movement of Americans who promote mental wellness for the health and well-being of the nation – everyday and in times of crisis.

www.mental-health-today.com

This website aims to reduce the tremendous amount of suffering people experience in their lives, with the knowledge that much of this suffering can be stopped. Many people are suffering today needlessly because most mental health care providers are mis-educated about many mental health disorders.

www.selfgrowth.com

Online self improvement community.

www.worldwidehealth.com

Worldwidehealth.com is an on-line Health Directory, bringing a central source of health related information covering many aspects of conventional to alternative and complementary therapy/medicine. It covers a wide range of topics ranging from Acupuncture to Yoga including 88 different categories, currently operating in six countries; United Kingdom, Ireland, United States of America, Canada, Australia and New Zealand.

www.sciencedaily.com

Science*Daily* is one of the Internet's most popular science news web sites. Since starting in 1995, the award-winning site has earned the loyalty of students, researchers, healthcare professionals, government agencies, educators and the general public around the world.

www.medicinenet.com

MedicineNet.com is an online, healthcare media publishing company. It provides easy-to-read, in-depth, authoritative medical information for consumers via its robust, user-friendly, interactive website.

Visit www.liggywebb.com for more information.

About The Author

Liggy Webb is widely respected as a leading expert in the field of Modern Life Skills. As a presenter, consultant and author she is passionate about her work and improving the quality of people's lives. She has developed a range of techniques and strategies to support individuals and organisations to cope more effectively and successfully with modern living and the demands and challenges of life in the twenty tens and beyond.

Contact liggy@liggywebb.com for more information.

Motivational Presentations
Liggy is noted for her dynamic and engaging style and as a result is frequently invited to present and speak at international conferences, award ceremonies, on board cruise ships, in the media and at a variety of high profile events.

Her experience and expertise is a blend of behavioural change, holistic health and positive psychology.

Contact info@liggywebb.com for more information.

Books & Publications

Liggy is the author of *How to Work Wonders - Your Guide to Workplace Wellness* and *The Happy Handbook - A Compendium of Modern Life Skills*

Her next book *Thank You - Your Guide to Appreciating Life* is due out in 2011.

Liggy is also Executive Editor for *Training Pages* - www.trainingages.com and writes for *People Alchemy* - www.peoplealchemy.co.uk. She is frequently asked to write for magazines and has a regular monthly column in *The Cheltonian* - www.thecheltonian.co.uk.

Consultancy

Liggy is a consultant for the United Nations and travels extensively working in a variety of worldwide locations. She is also the founding director of The Learning Architect, an international learning and development organisation. Visit www.thelearningarchitect.com

Charity

Liggy is a trustee of The Chrysalis Foundation (www.chrysalisprogramme.com) and actively supports mental health charities.

* * * * * *

This Life

If you could view your whole life what would it be

If your religion was kindness, could you say that was me

Were your days on this earth blessed with loving and living

Could you honestly say, there was less taking than giving

The people you've loved, did they know that you did

Or for fear of rejection were your feelings well hid

Did you love to your limit and embrace with your heart

When the clouds blocked the sun did you trust they'd part

Did you dance with the angels at night in your dreams

Was your courage enough to reach for sunbeams

When those souls that you loved were bereft and alone

Was your kindness enough to offer all that you own

Did you live your life truly through your past and beyond

Did your lilies of enlightenment surface your pond

If you could view your whole life what would it be

If your past was a vision would you like what you see

© Liggy Webb